BigTime® Piano

Rock 'n Roll

2011 Edition

Level 4

Intermediate

Arranged by

Nancy and Randall Faber

Production Coordinator: Jon Ophoff
Design and Illustration: Terpstra Design, San Francisco
Engraving: Dovetree Productions, Inc.

3042 Creek Drive
Ann Arbor, Michigan 48108

A NOTE TO TEACHERS

BigTime® Piano Rock 'n Roll allows the pianist to "let go" and enjoy the fun sounds of the '50s, '60s and '70s. Upbeat rhythms and pianistic arrangements make the book a delight for both students and teachers. New selections include *Great Balls of Fire*, *I Heard It Through the Grapevine*, Carole King's *I Feel the Earth Move*, and more.

BigTime® Piano Rock 'n Roll is part of the *BigTime® Piano* series arranged by Faber and Faber. "BigTime" designates Level 4 of the *PreTime® to BigTime® Supplementary Library*. The *BigTime® Piano* series is arranged for the intermediate pianist and it marks a significant achievement for the piano student. As the name implies, "BigTime" selections and arrangements are designed to be fun, showy, and to inspire enthusiasm and pride in the piano student.

Following are the levels of the supplementary library, which lead from *PreTime®* to *BigTime®*.

PreTime® Piano	(Primer Level)
PlayTime® Piano	(Level 1)
ShowTime® Piano	(Level 2A)
ChordTime® Piano	(Level 2B)
FunTime® Piano	(Level 3A – 3B)
BigTime® Piano	(Level 4)

Each level offers books in a variety of styles, making it possible for the teacher to offer stimulating material for every student. For a complimentary detailed listing, e-mail faber@pianoadventures.com or write us at the address below.

Visit **www.PianoAdventures.com**.

Helpful Hints:

1. Music is social, too. Students who memorize a couple of songs from this book are always ready to share at parties and for friends.
2. As rhythm is of prime importance, encourage the student to feel the rhythm in his/her body when playing music. This can be accomplished with the tapping of the toe or heel, and with clapping exercises.
3. The songs can be assigned in any order. Selection is usually best made by the student, according to interest and enthusiasm.
4. Chord symbols are given above the treble staff. Time taken to help the student see how chords are used in the arrangement is time well spent. Such work can help memory, sight-reading, and even help the student build improvisation, composition and arranging skills.

About Rock 'n Roll

The beat of rock and roll captured the spirit of the youth and the attention of the music industry in the '50s. With its upbeat rhythm, rock 'n roll proved irresistible to all young people.

Pioneers such as Chuck Berry, Fats Domino, and Little Richard led the way for the rock 'n roll king — Elvis Presley. Other greats such as Bill Haley, Carl Perkins, and the legendary Jerry Lee Lewis made significant contributions to the new music form. Bolstered by the rise of celebrity disc jockeys and Dick Clark's "American Bandstand" on television, the sound spread quickly throughout the U.S. and soon to Britain. There it was picked up by The Beatles and The Rolling Stones who, in the '60s, went on to usher in yet another rock era.

ISBN 978-1-61677-029-7

TABLE OF CONTENTS

Rock Around the Clock

Words by
MAX C. FREEDMAN

Music by
JIMMY DeKNIGHT

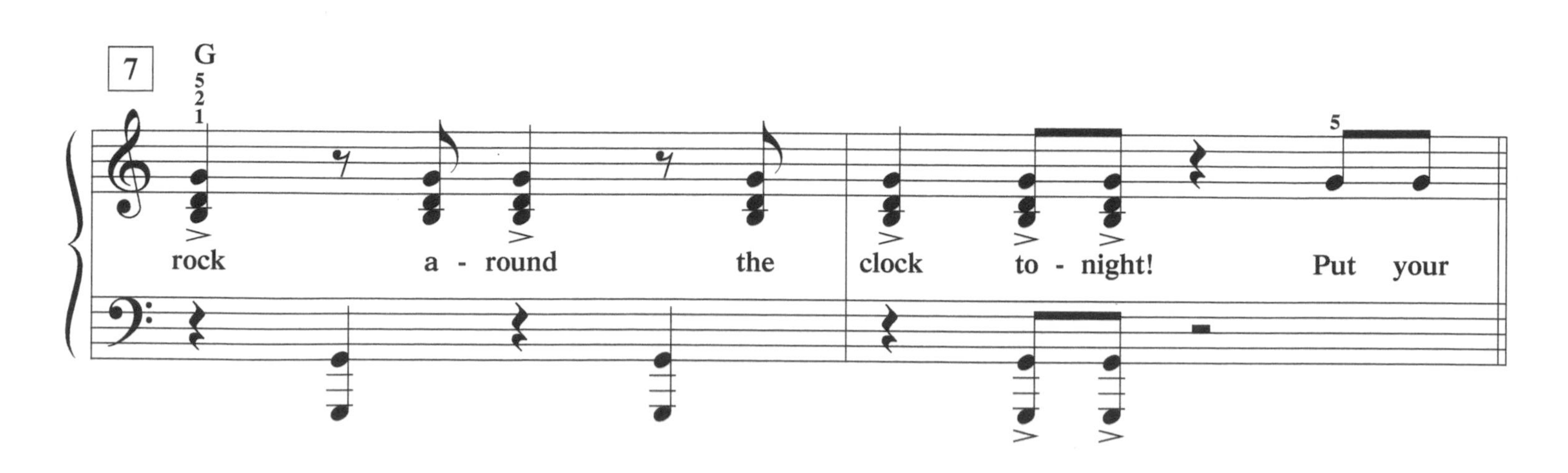

9
C
glad rags on, join me hon', gon - na have some fun when (the)
clock strikes two, three and four, and the band slows down we'll

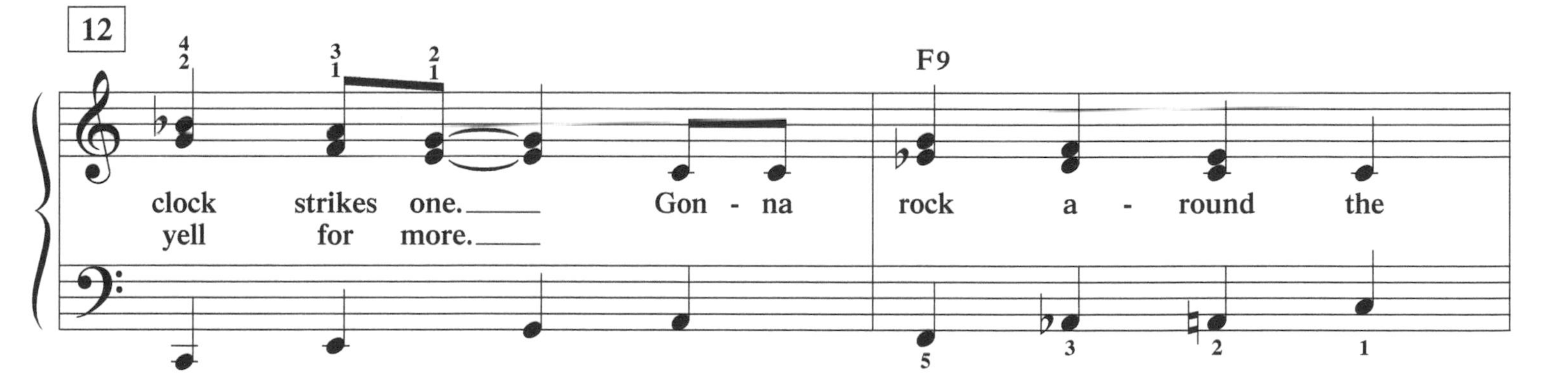
12
F9
clock strikes one. Gon - na rock a - round the
yell for more.

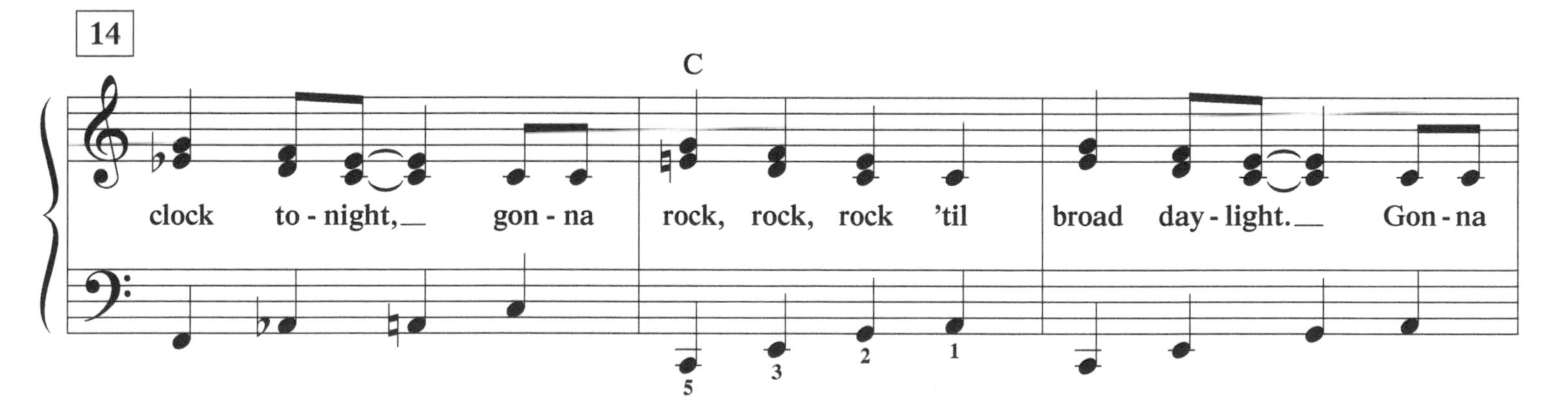
14
C
clock to - night, gon - na rock, rock, rock 'til broad day - light. Gon - na

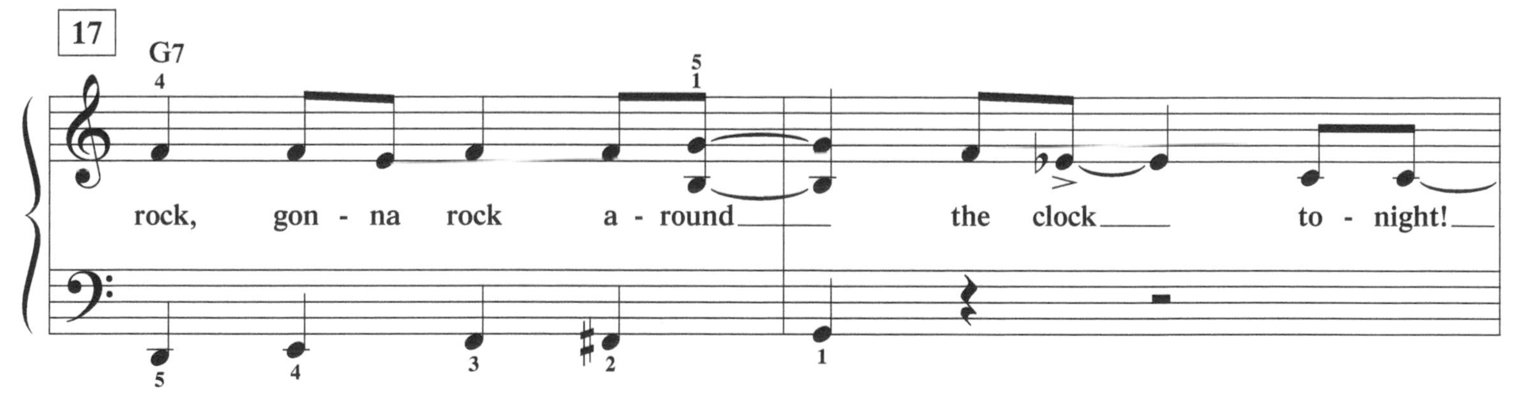
17
G7
rock, gon - na rock a - round the clock to - night!

19
C6
1.
When the
2.

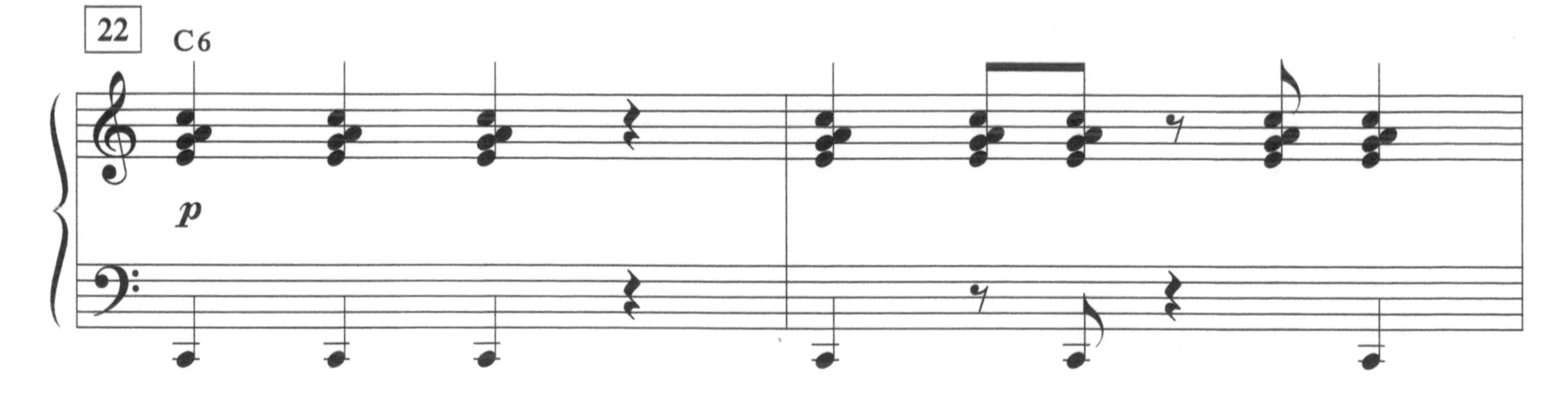
22
C6
p

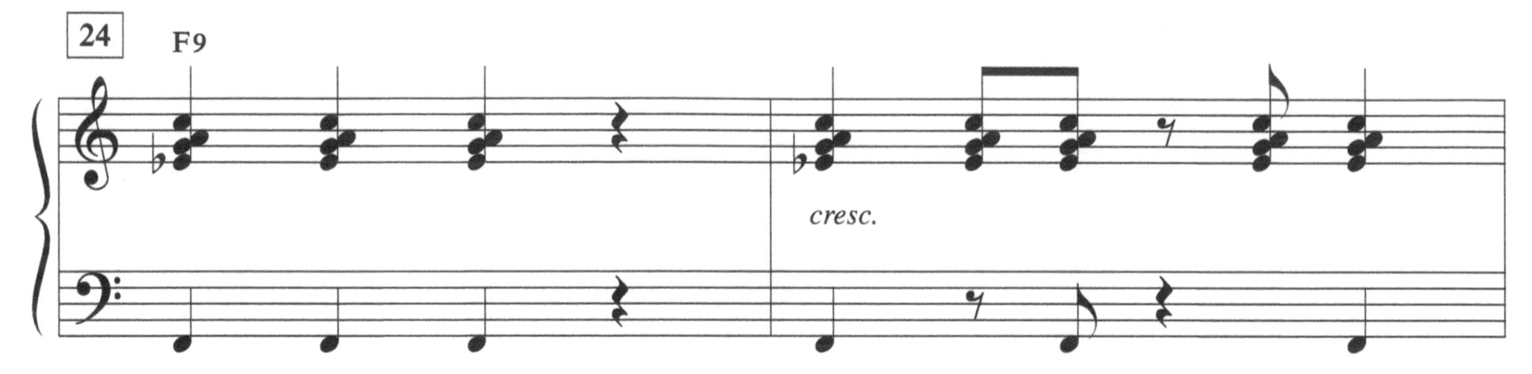
24
F9
cresc.

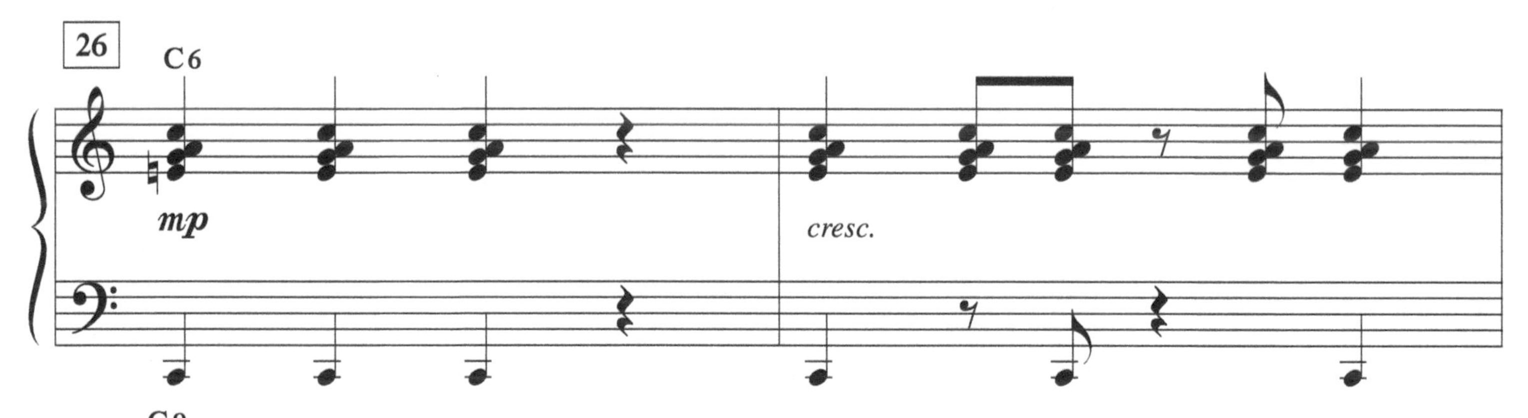
26
C6
mp
cresc.

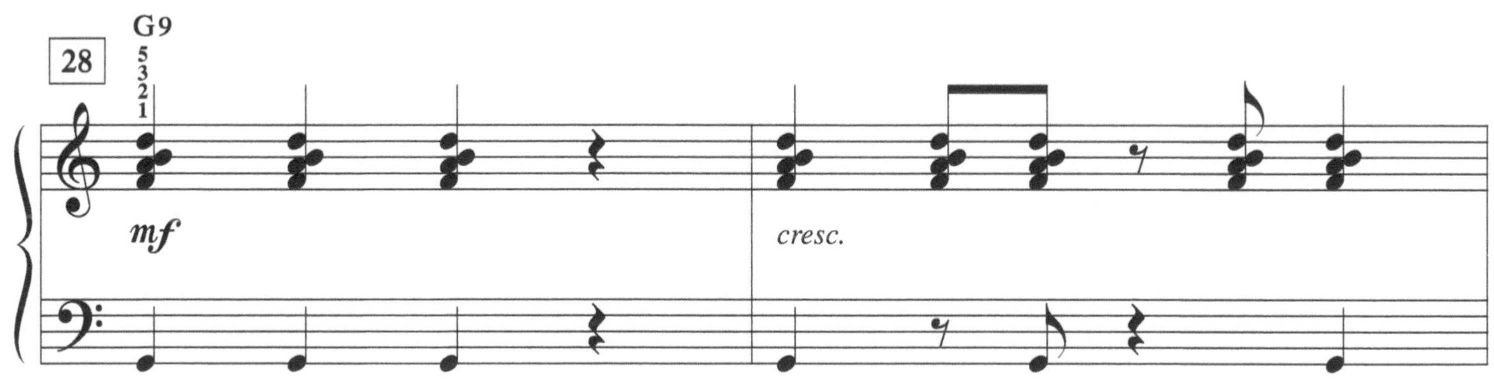
G9
28
5
3
2
1
mf
cresc.

30
C6
f
5
When the
mf

32
C
chimes ring five,
six, and sev'n,
we'll be right in

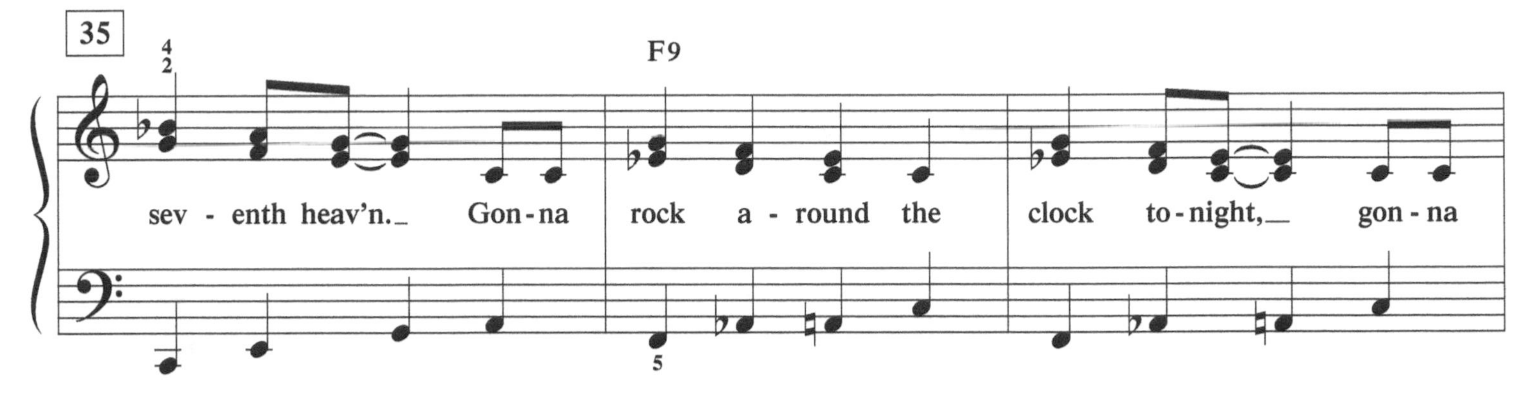
35
F9
sev - enth heav'n. Gon - na
rock a - round the
clock to - night, gon - na

38
C
G7
rock, rock, rock 'til
broad day - light. Gon - na
rock, gon - na rock a - round

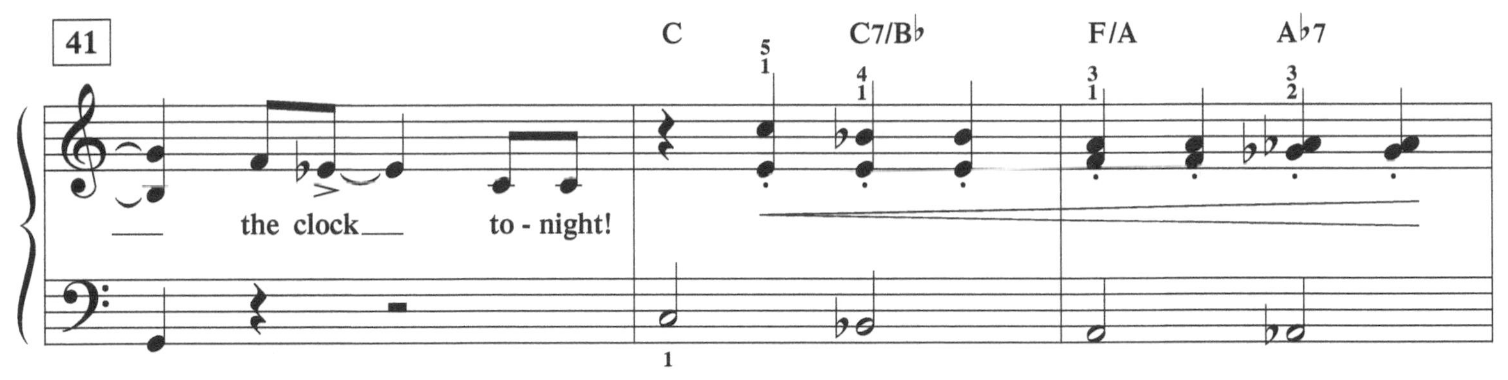
41
C
C7/B♭
F/A
A♭7
the clock to - night!

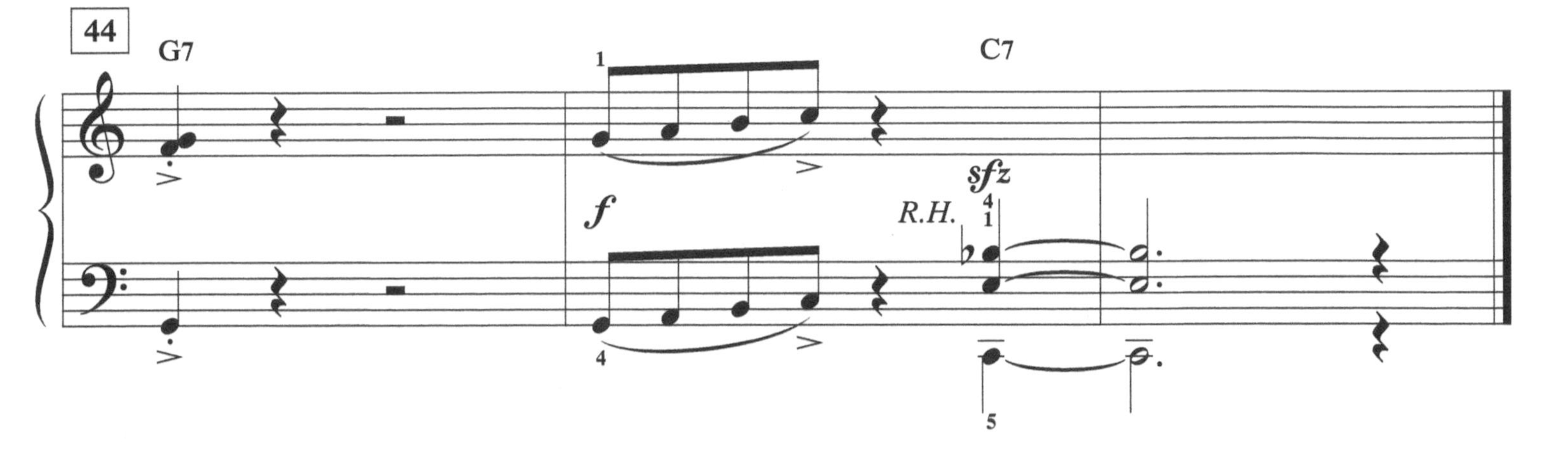
44
G7
C7
f
R.H.
sfz

Piano Man

Words and Music by
BILLY JOEL

17
G/C
F
C
C/B
mf
He says, "Son, can you play me a
He says, "Bill, I be - lieve this is

21
C/A
C/G
F
C/E
mem - o - ry? I'm not real - ly sure how it
kill - ing me," as a smile ran a - way from his

25
D7
G
C
C/B
goes, but it's sad and it's sweet and I
face. "Well I'm sure that I could be a

29
C/A
C/G
F
F/G
knew it com - plete when I wore a young - er man's
mo - vie star if I could get out of this

33
C
Am
Am/G
clothes."
place."
Da da da de de
mp

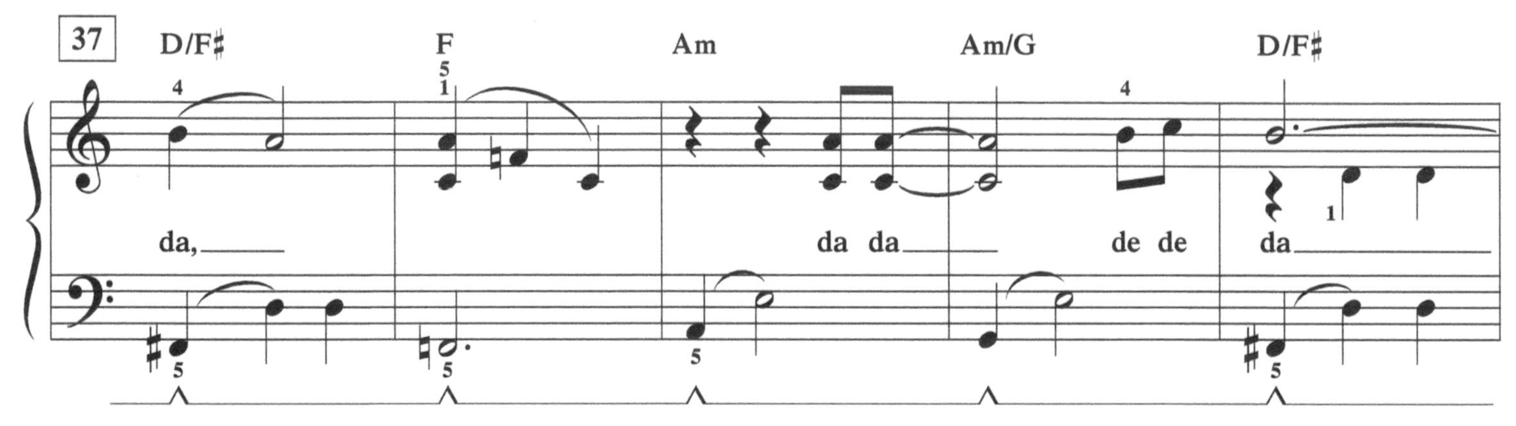
37
D/F♯
F
Am
Am/G
D/F♯
da,
da da
de de
da

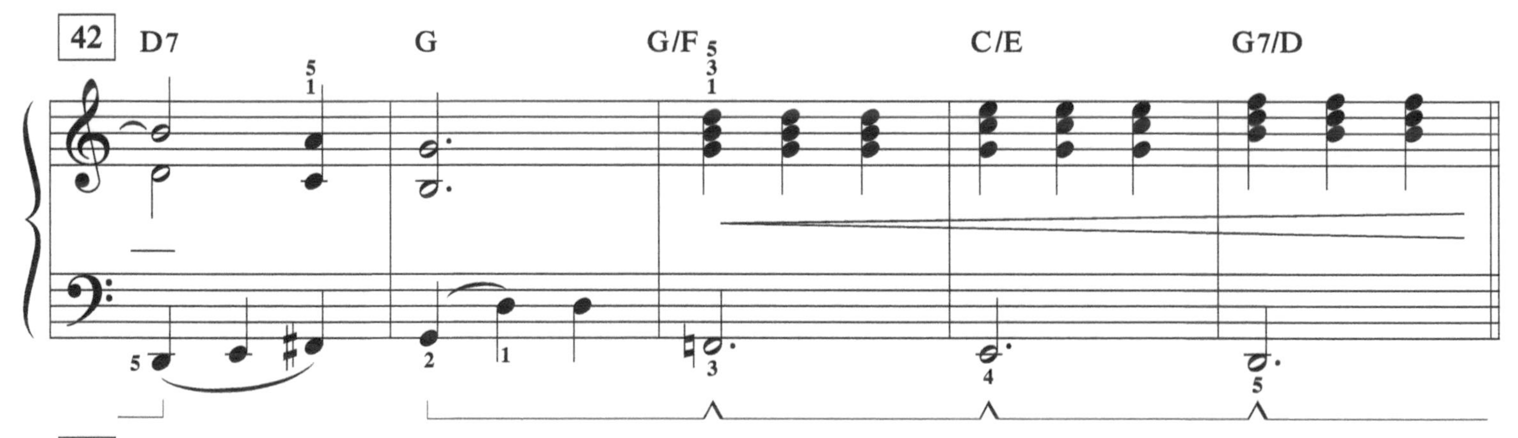
42
D7
G
G/F
C/E
G7/D

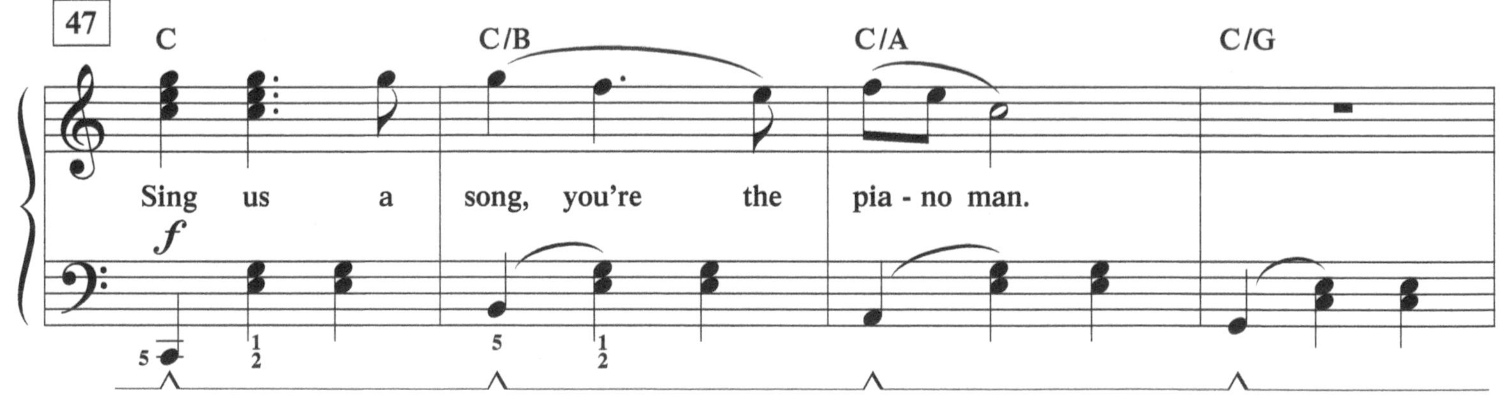
47
C
C/B
C/A
C/G
Sing us a song, you're the pia - no man.
f

51
F
C/E
D
G
Sing us a song to - night.
Well, we're

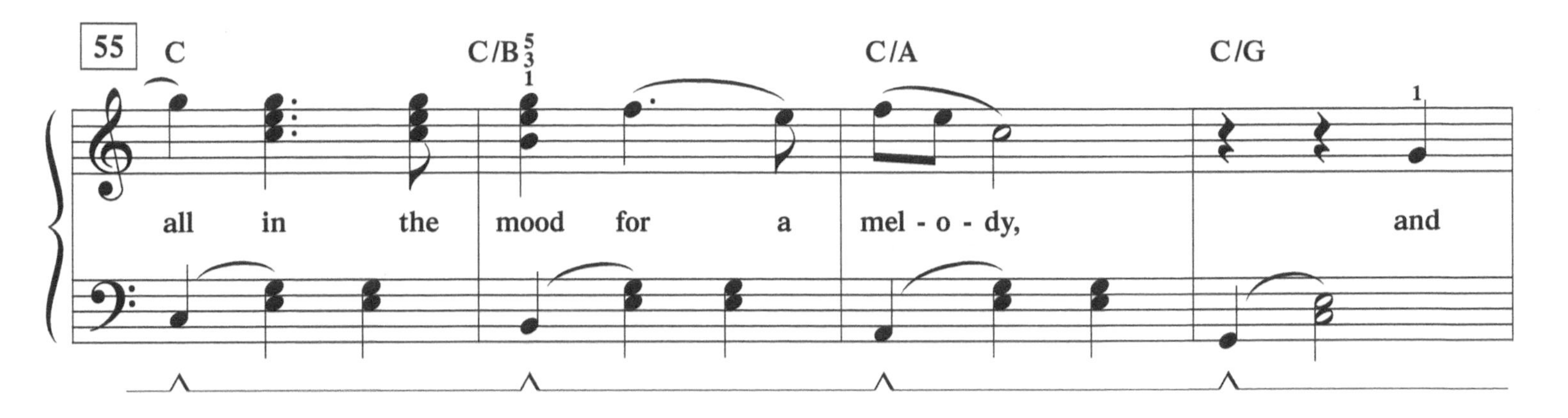

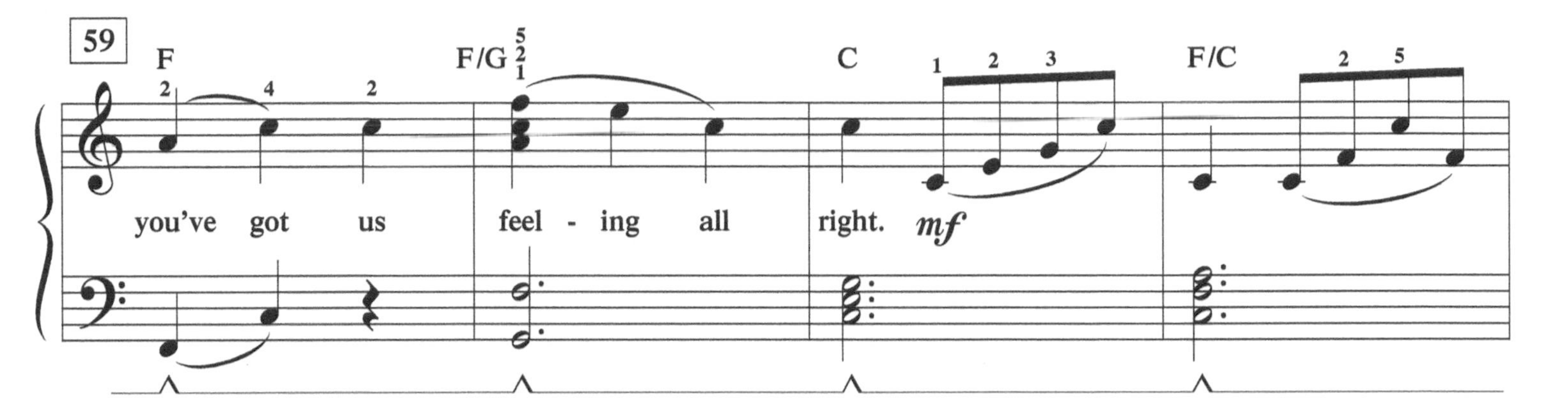

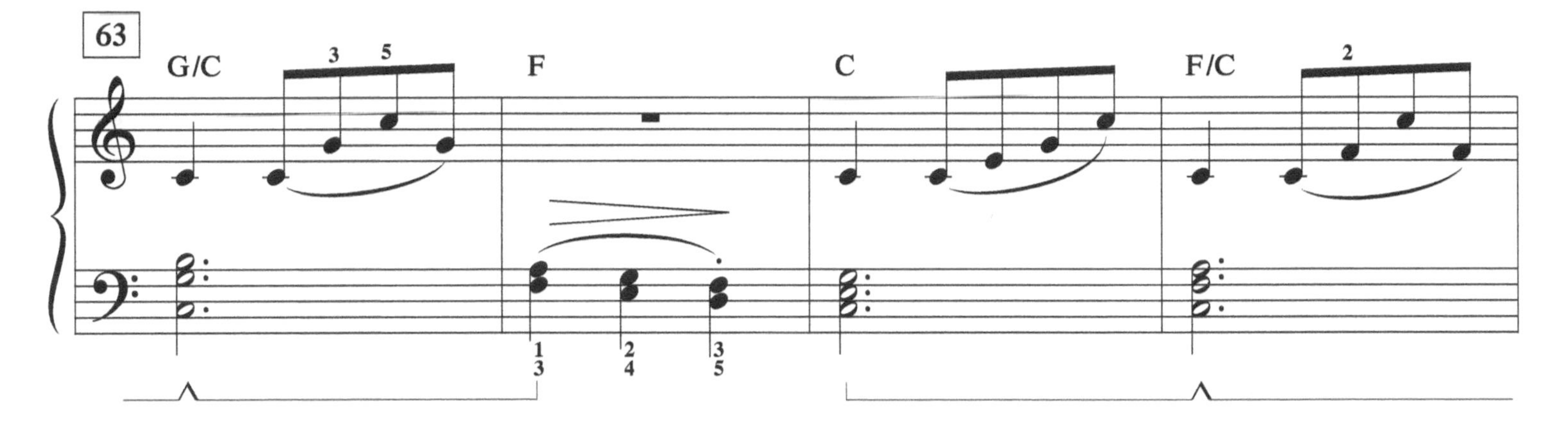

Additional Lyrics

3. Now Paul is a real estate novelist,
who never had time for a wife,
and he's talkin' with Davy, who's still in the Navy
and probably will be for life.
And the waitress is practicing politics
as the businessmen slowly get stoned.
Yes, they're sharing a drink they call loneliness,
but it's better than drinkin' alone.

4. It's a pretty good crowd for a Saturday,
and the manager gives me a smile
'cause he knows that it's me they've been comin' to see
to forget about life for awhile.
And the piano sounds like a carnival,
and the microphone smells like a beer,
and they sit at the bar and put bread in my jar
and say, "Man, what are you doin' here?"

Strawberry Malt

NANCY FABER

Cheerfully, with a swing

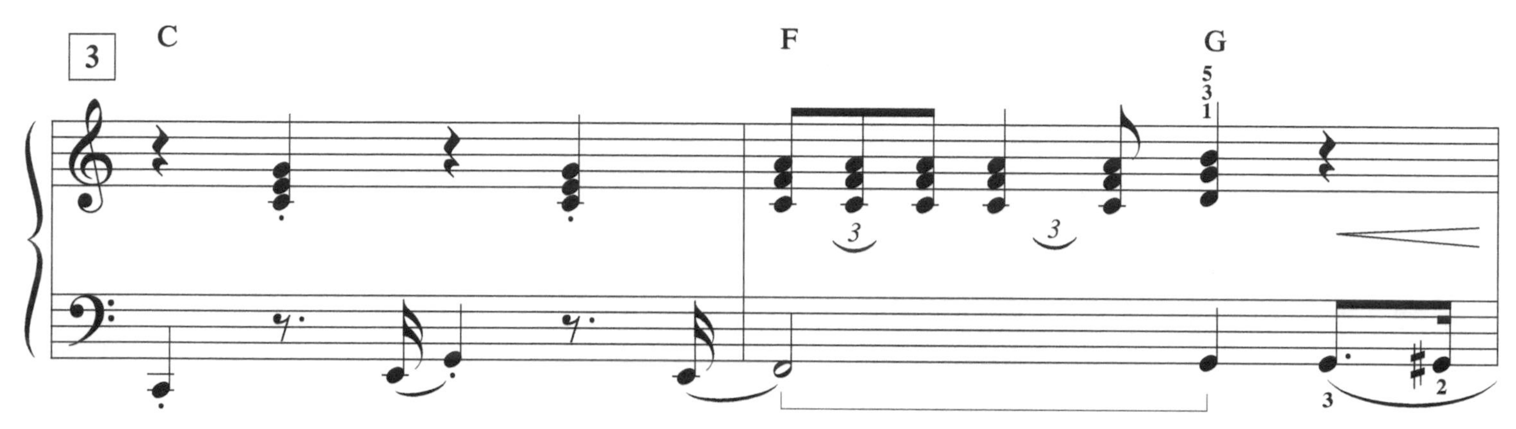

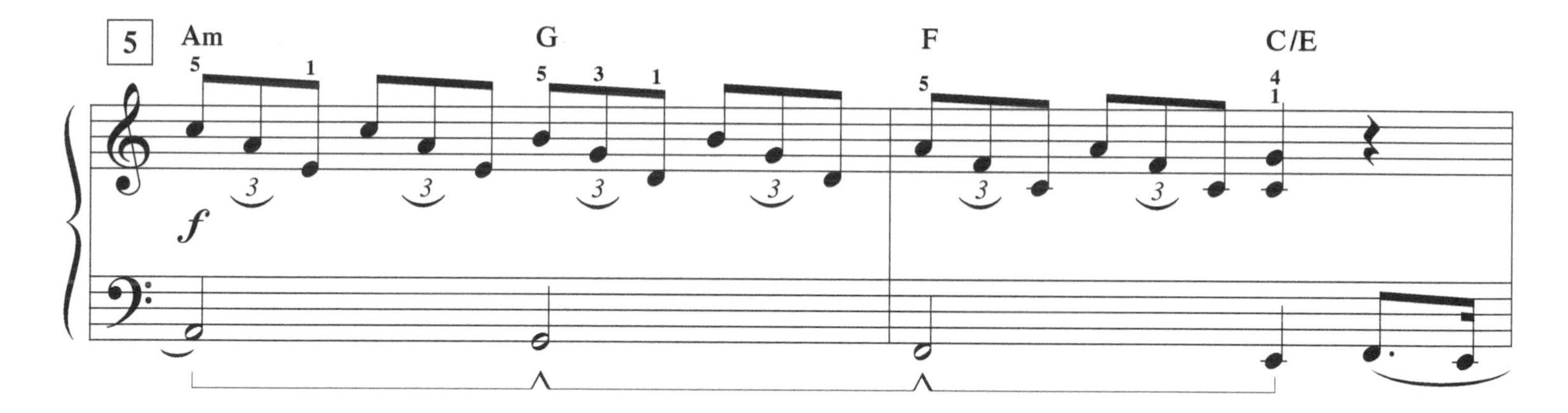

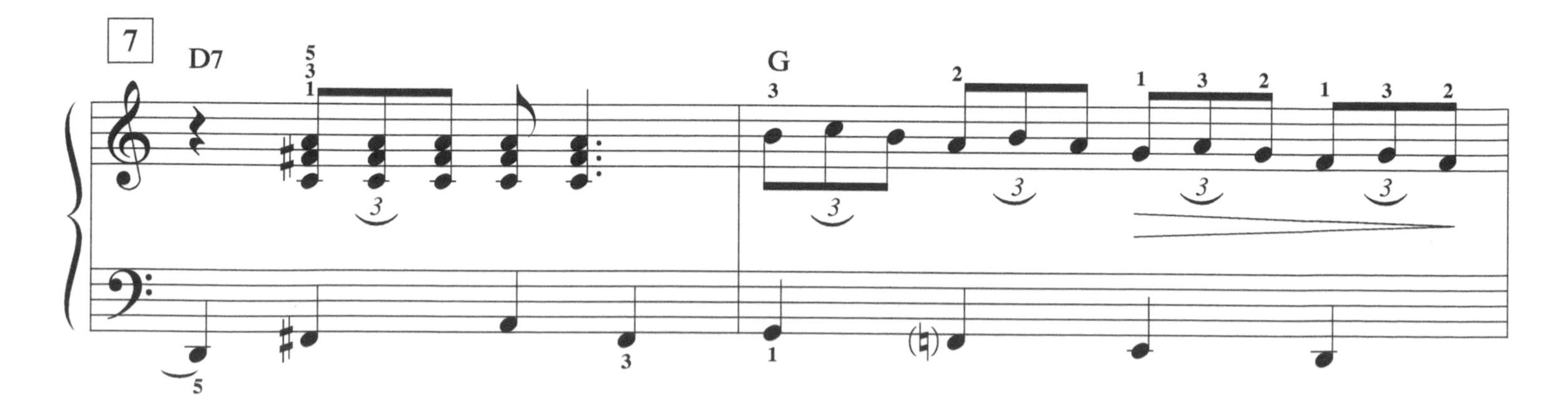

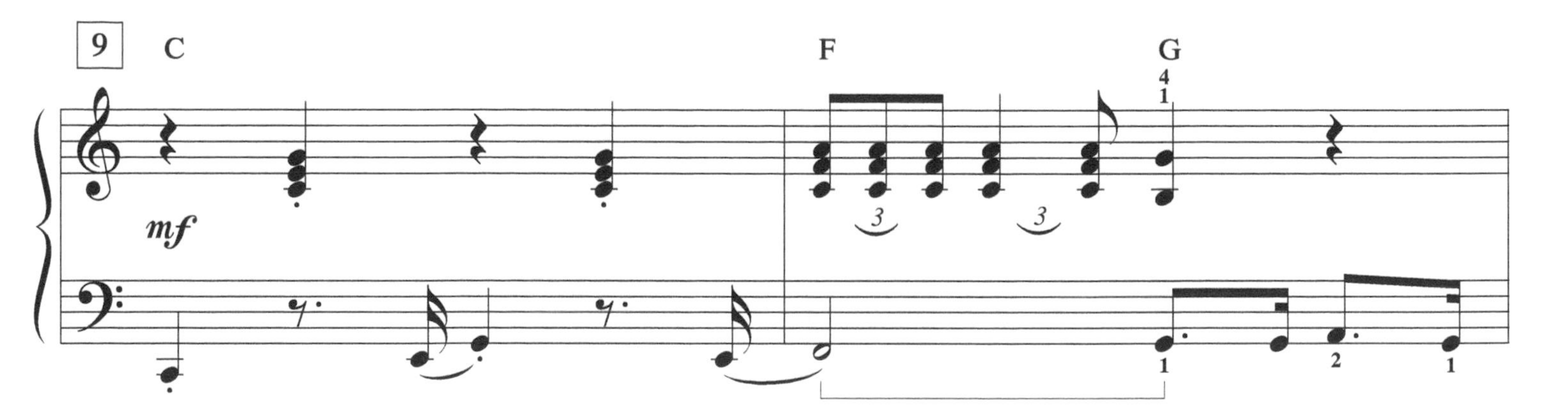
9
C
F
G
mf

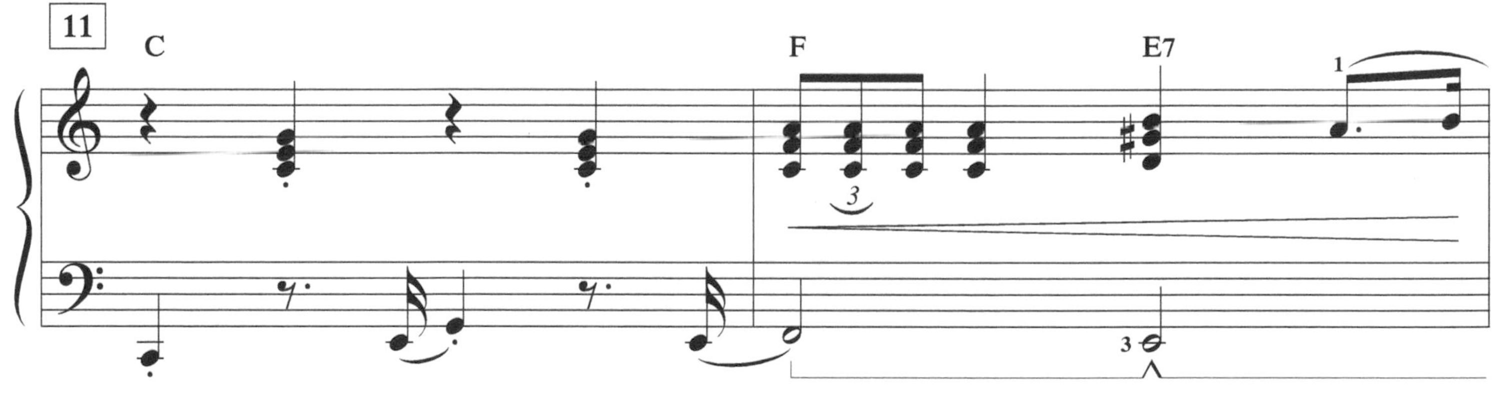
11
C
F
E7

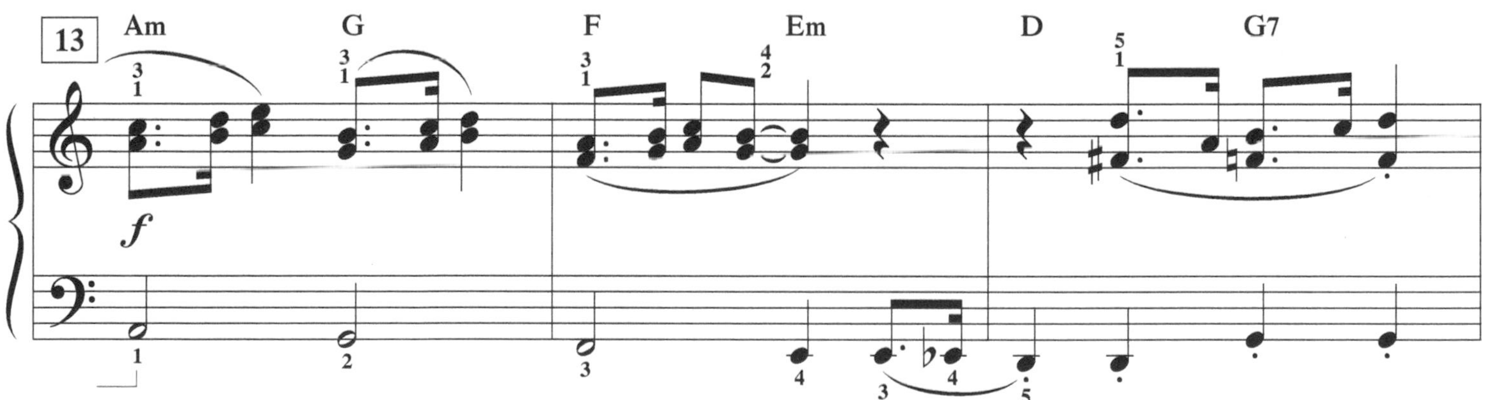
13
Am
G
F
Em
D
G7
f

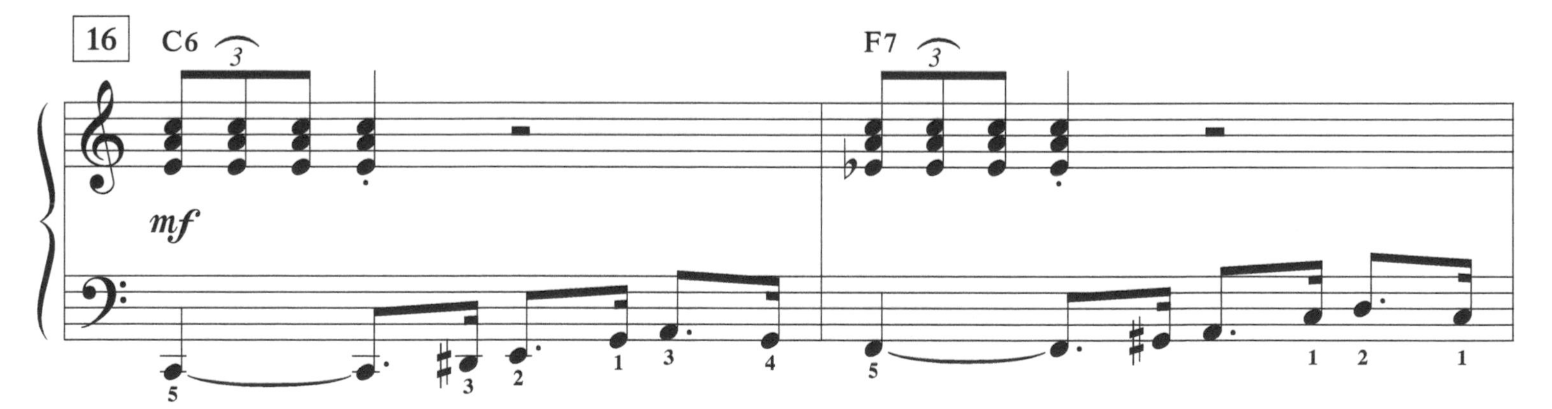
16
C6
F7
mf

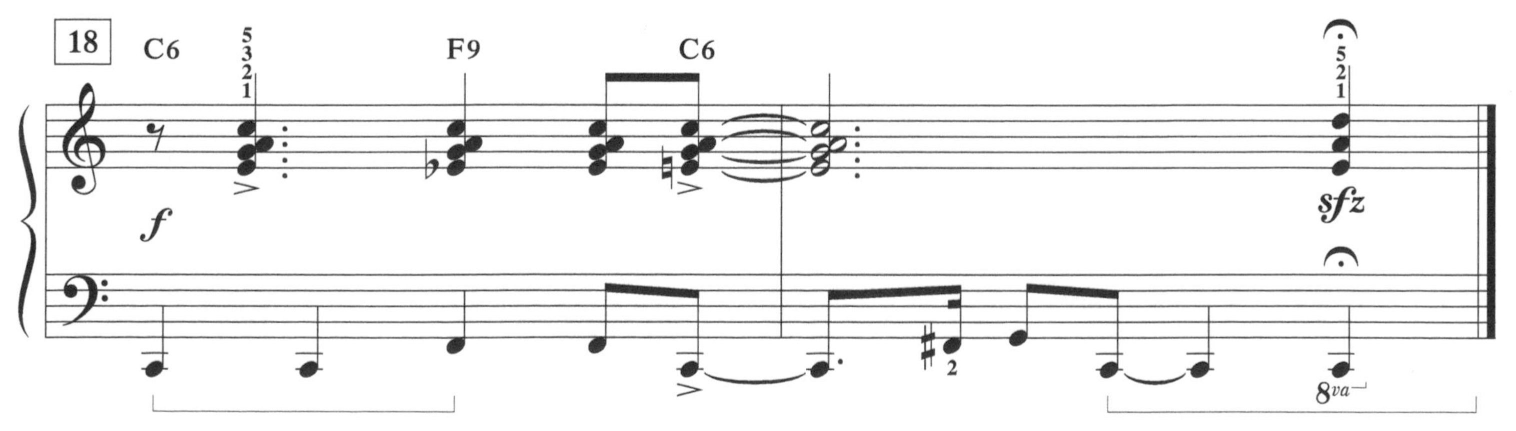
18
C6
F9
C6
f
sfz
8va

My Special Angel

Words and Music by
JIMMY DUNCAN

Moderately slow, with a swing

C Am F G7

8va (optional)

3 (8va)

C Am F G7

5 C Am Em

You are my spe - cial an - gel,

7 F G C

sent from up a - bove.

9 F G C Am D7

The Lord smiled down on me and sent an an - gel to

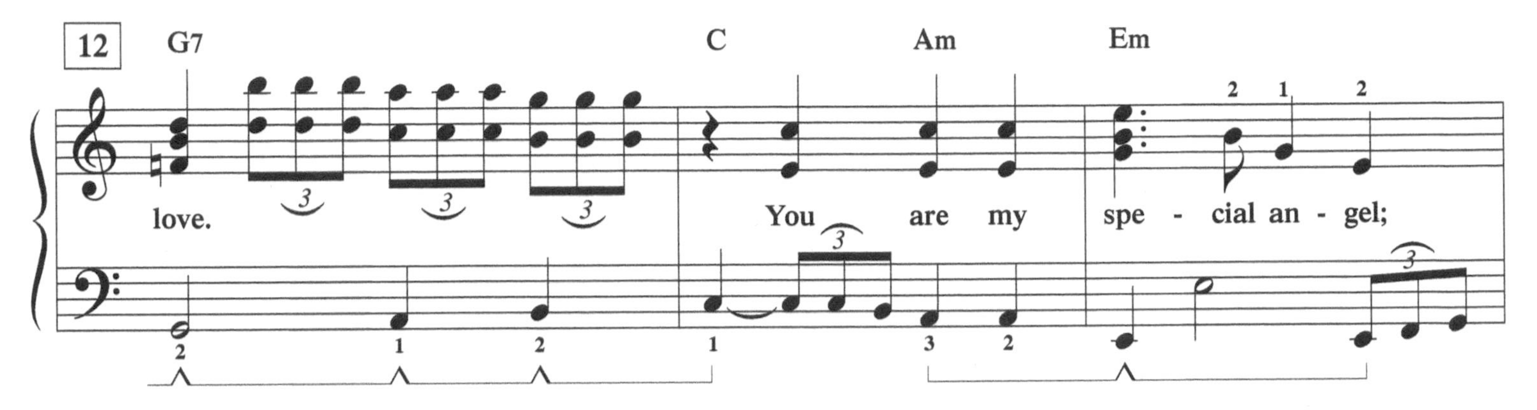
12
G7
C
Am
Em
love.
You are my
spe - cial an - gel;

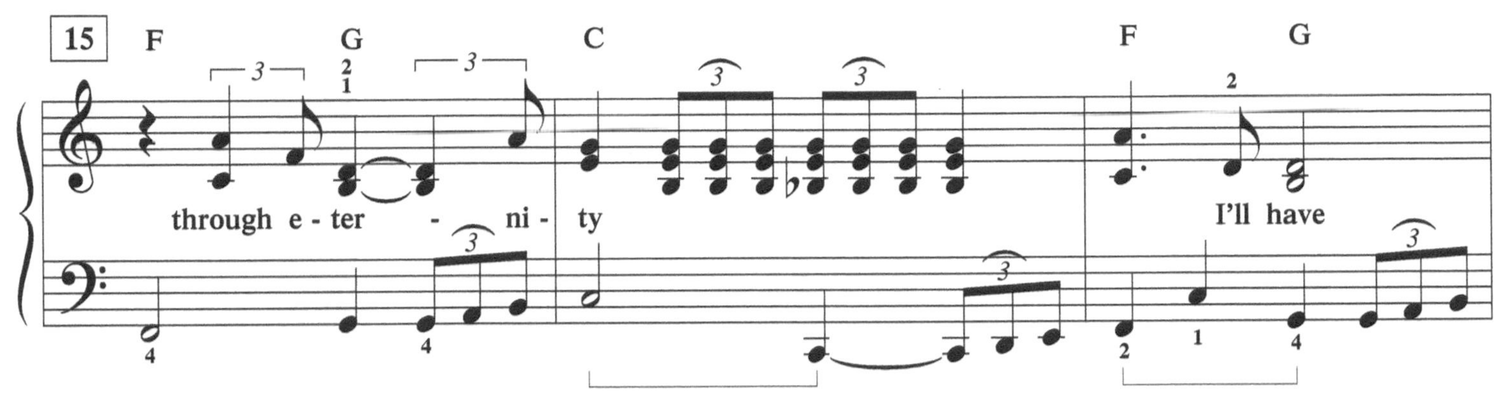
15
F
G
C
F
G
through e - ter - ni - ty
I'll have

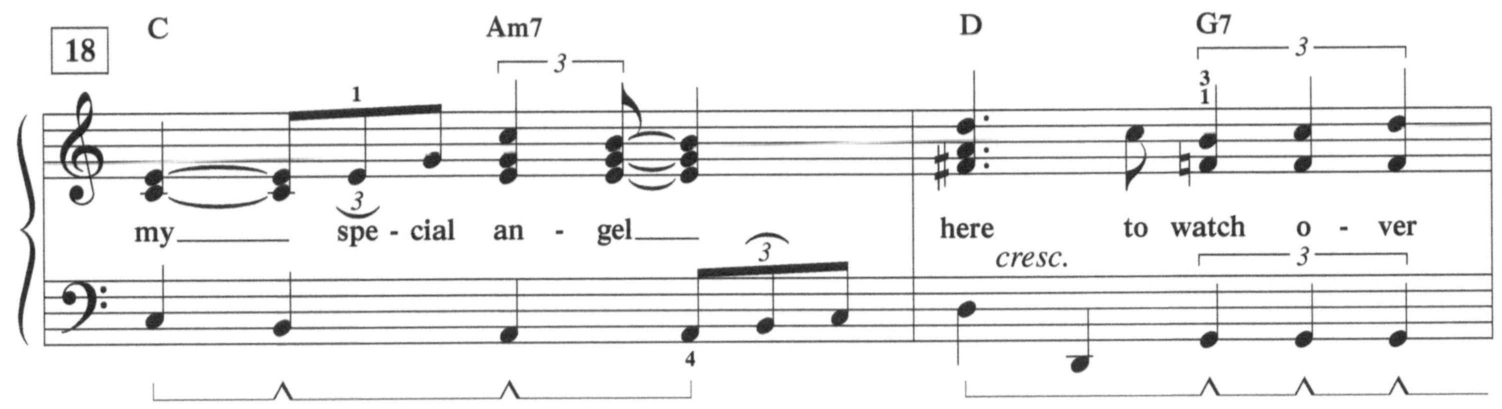
18
C
Am7
D
G7
my spe - cial an - gel
here to watch o - ver
cresc.

20
E
A7
Dm
G7
me,
here to watch o - ver
f
mf
molto rit.

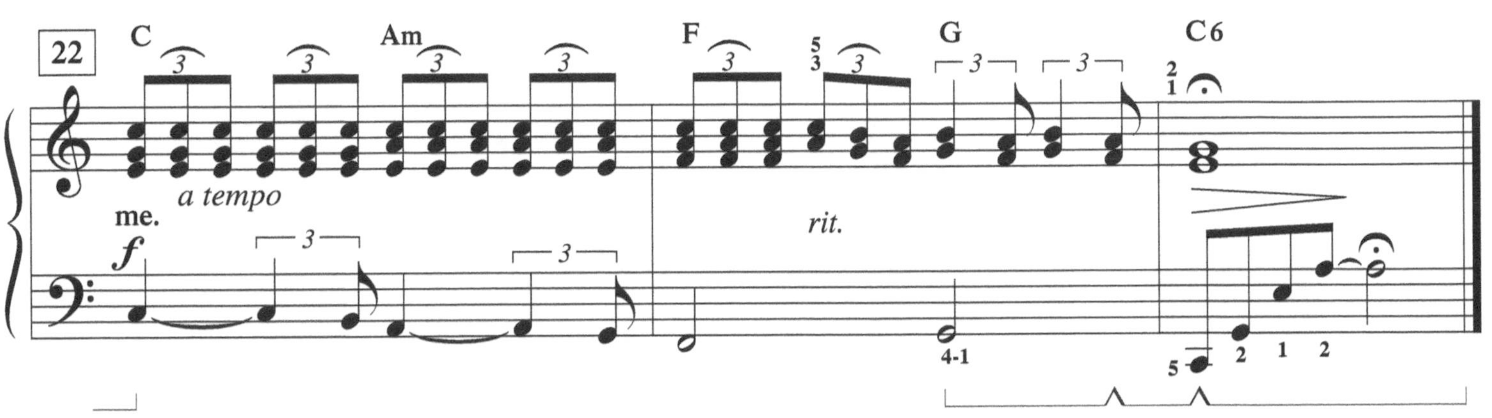
22
C
Am
F
G
C6
me.
a tempo
f
rit.

When a Man Loves a Woman

Words and Music by
CALVIN LEWIS and ANDREW WRIGHT

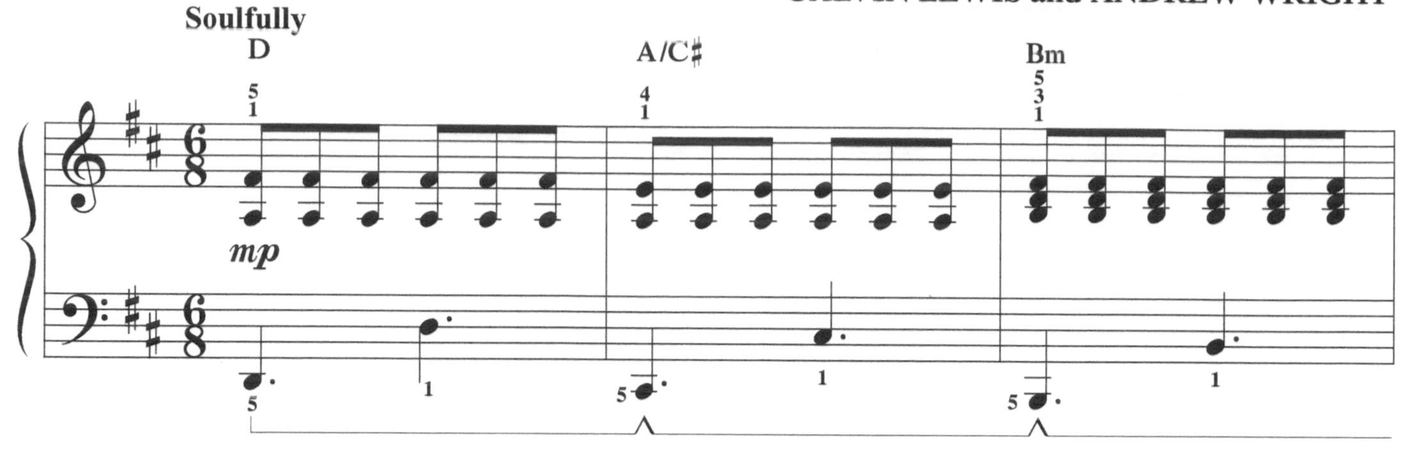

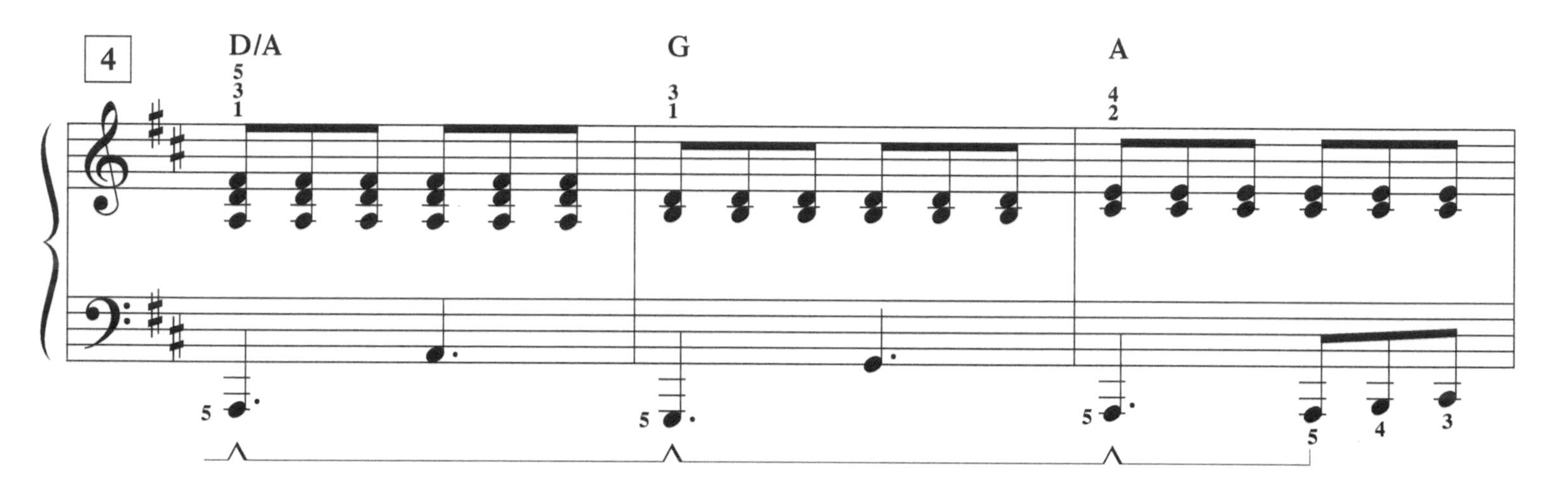

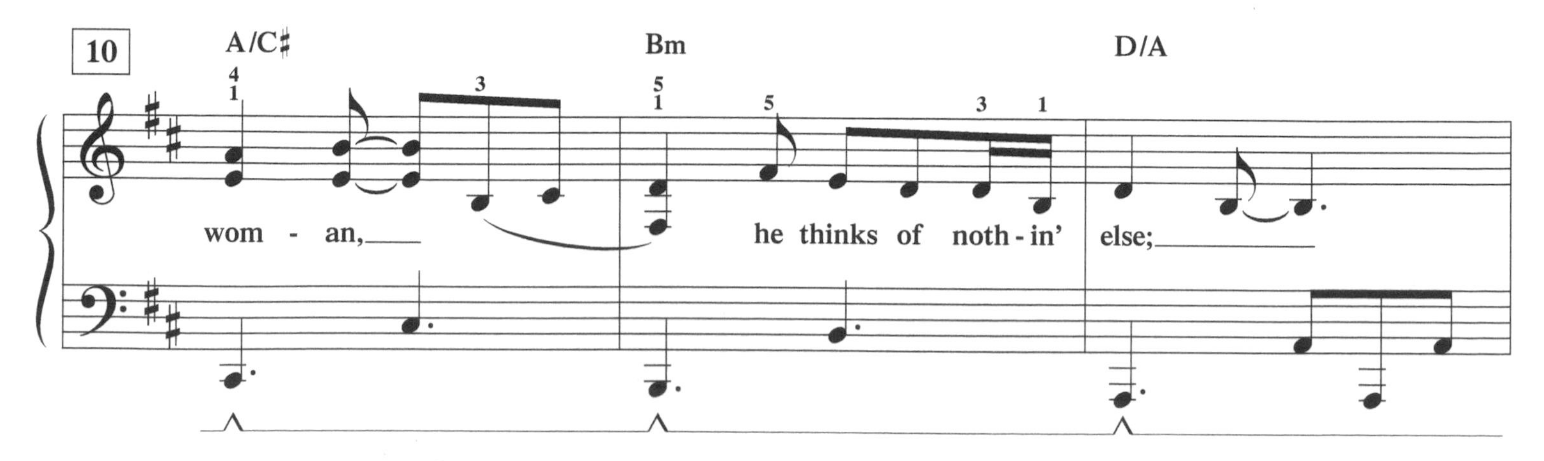

13
G
A
D
he'd change the world for the good thing he's found.
16
A
D
A/C♯
If she's bad he can't see it,
Ped. simile
19
Bm
D/A
G
she can do no wrong;
turn his back on his best
22
A
D
D7
friend if he put her down.
25
G
D
Well, this man loves you, wom - an;

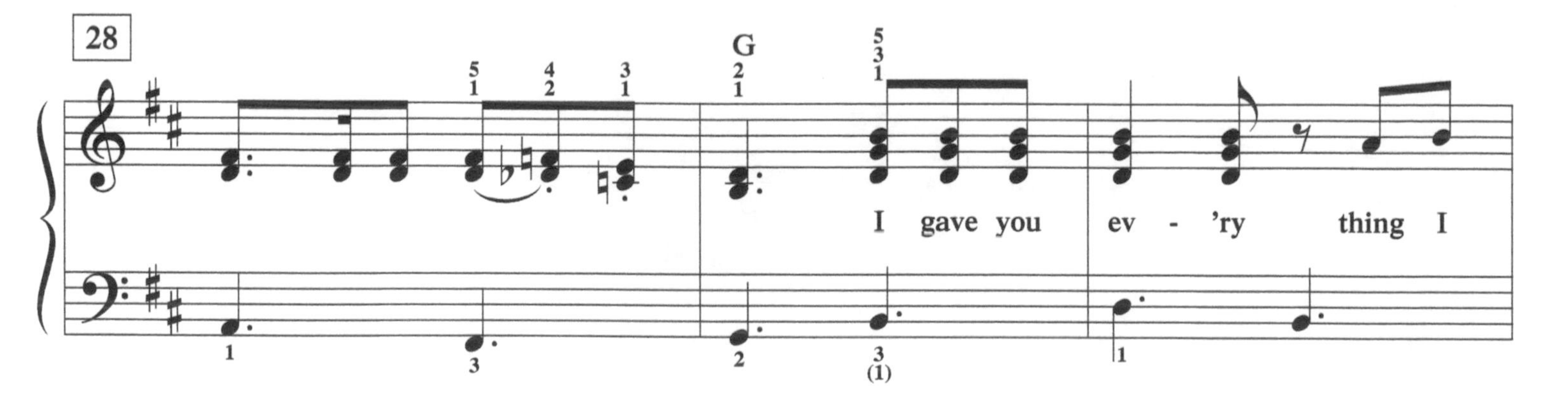
28
G
I gave you ev - 'ry thing I

31
D
G
had.
Try - in' to

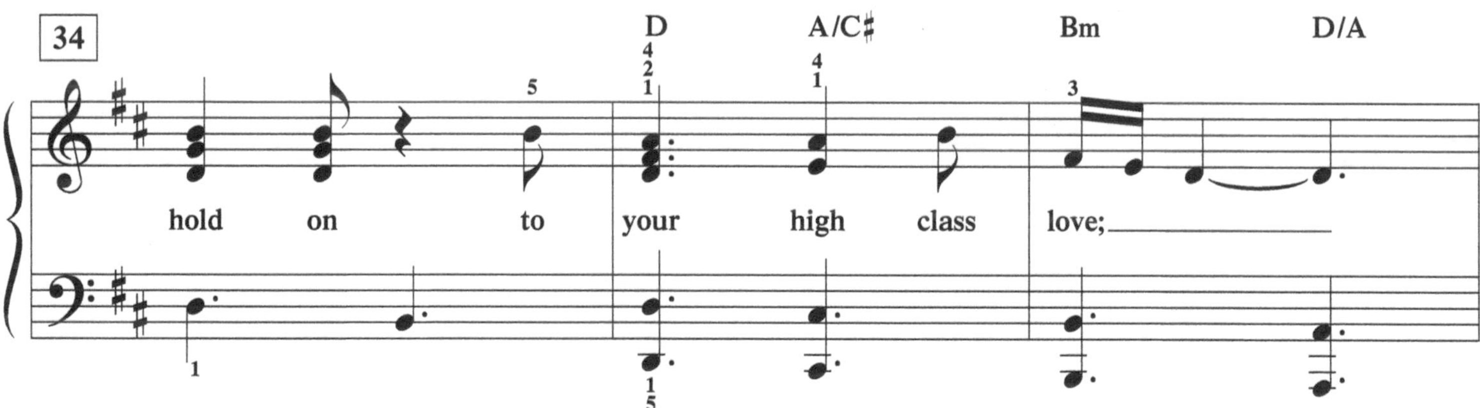
34
D
A/C♯
Bm
D/A
hold on to your high class love;

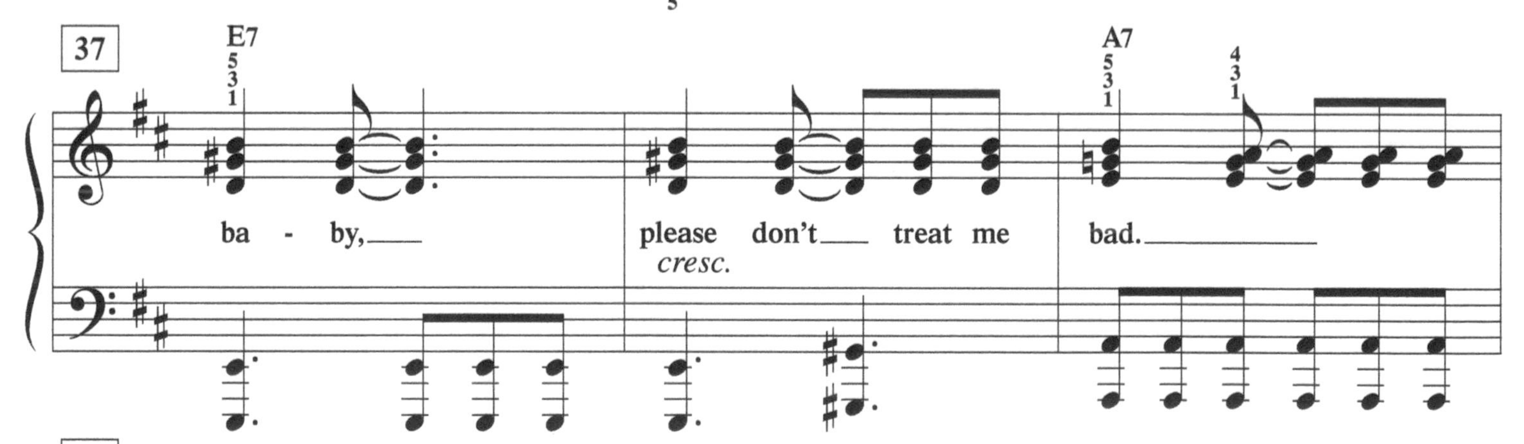
37
E7
A7
ba - by,
please don't treat me bad.
cresc.

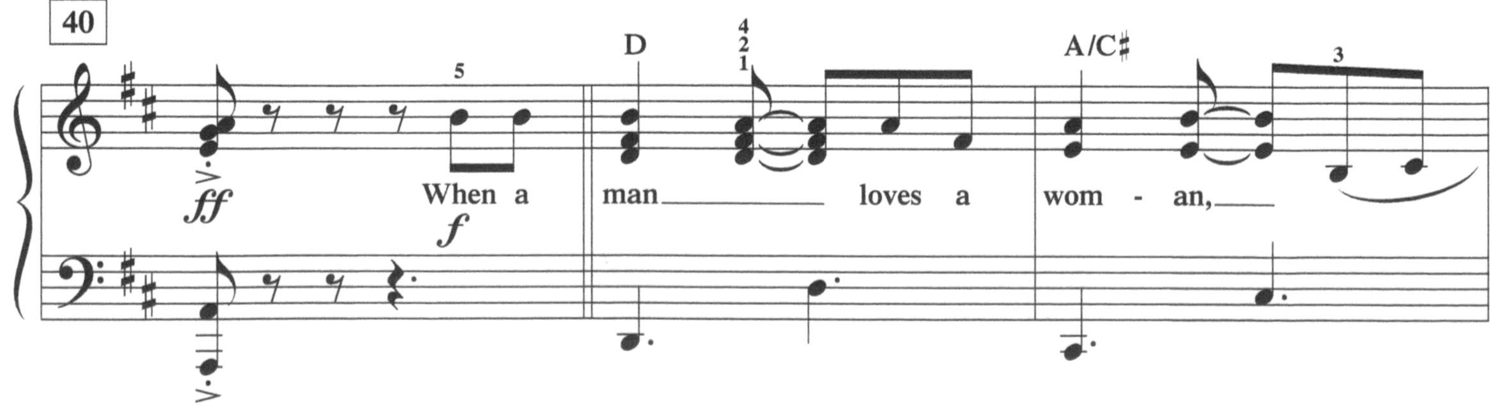
40
D
A/C♯
When a man loves a wom - an,
ff
f

43
Bm
D/A
G
he could nev - er do her wrong;
he'd nev - er

46
A
D
A
want some oth - er girl.
When a

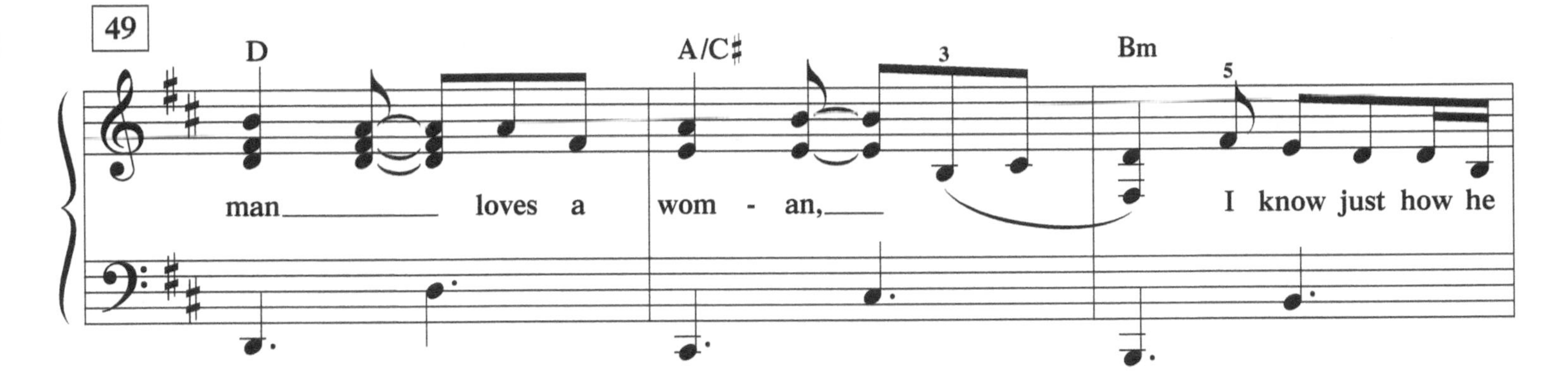
49
D
A/C♯
Bm
man loves a wom - an,
I know just how he

52
D/A
G
A
feels,
'cause, ba - by, ba - by, you're my

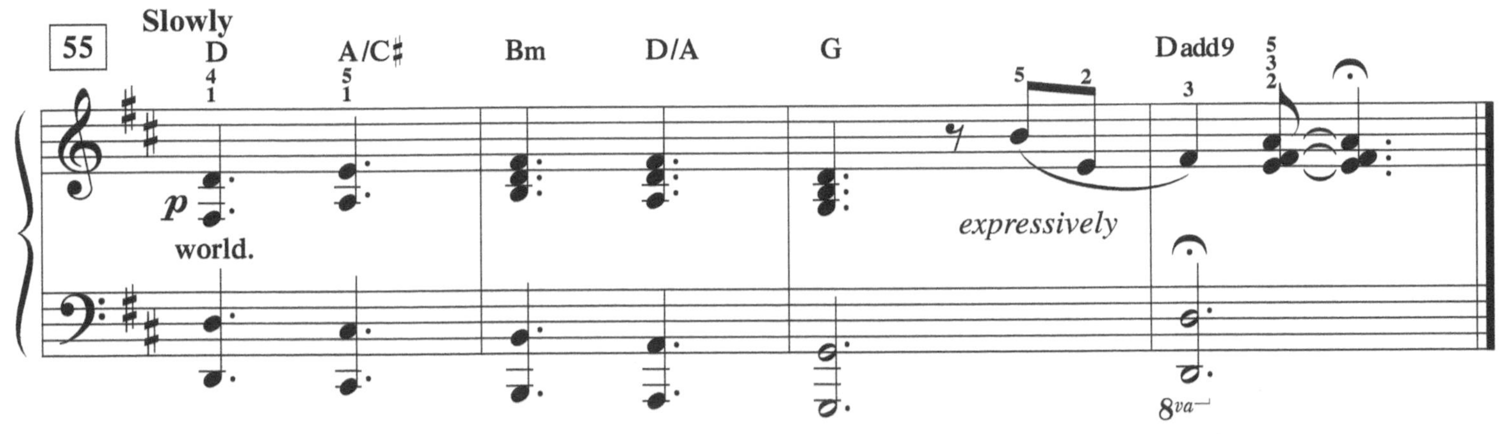
Slowly
55
D
A/C♯
Bm
D/A
G
Dadd9
p
world.
expressively
8va

Great Balls of Fire

Words and Music by
OTIS BLACKWELL and JACK HAMMER

11
F7
G7
You came a-long and you moved me, hon-ey. I changed my mind,
mp

14
F7
C7
L.H.
love's just fine. Good-ness gra-cious, great balls of fire!
f
8va

17
F9
C
Kiss me, ba-by. Woo...

20
F9
8va
gliss.
Hold me, ba-by.

23
G7
I want to love you like a lov - er should.
You're fine,
mp

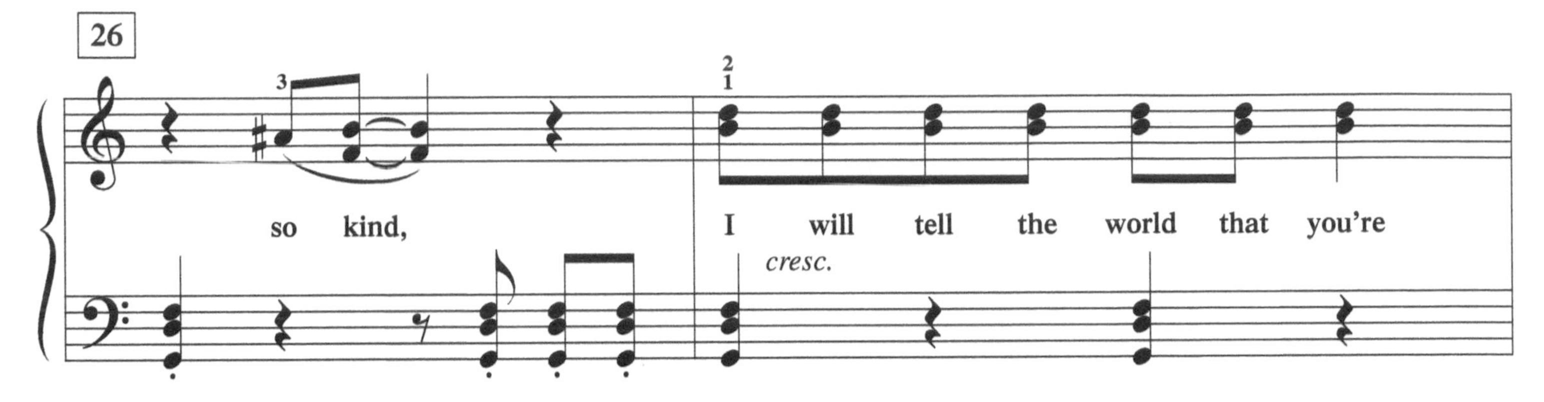
26
so kind,
I will tell the world that you're
cresc.

28
C7
mine, mine, mine, mine!
f
I chew my nails and I twid-dle my thumb.
mf

31
F7
I'm real ner-vous, but it sure is fun.
G7
Come on, ba - by,
mp
34
F7
you drive me cra - zy.
C7
L.H.
Good - ness gra - cious, great balls of fire!
ff
8va
8va

I Heard It Through the Grapevine

Words and Music by
NORMAN J. WHITFIELD and BARRETT STRONG

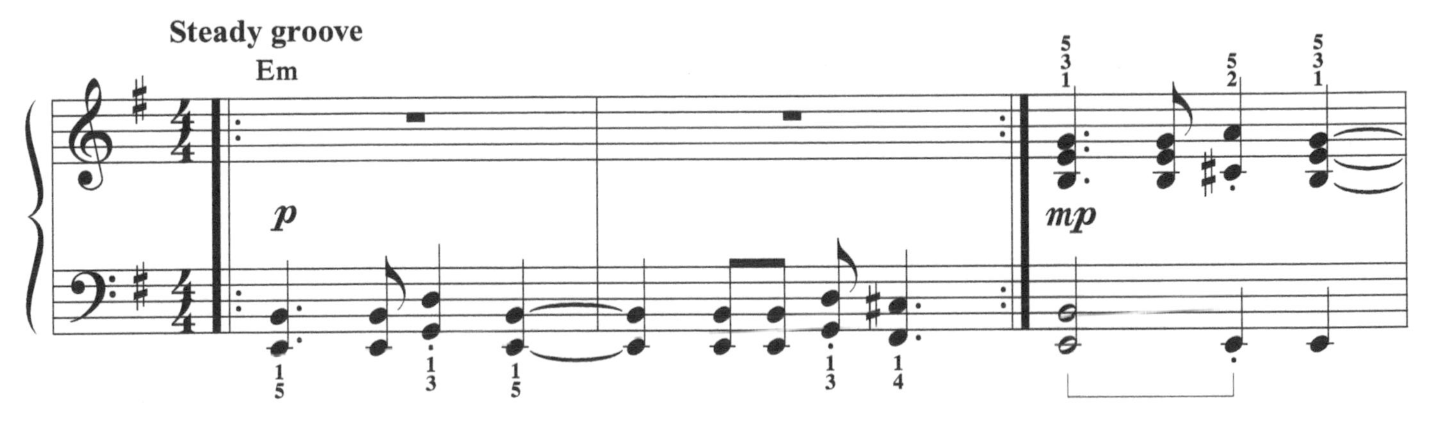

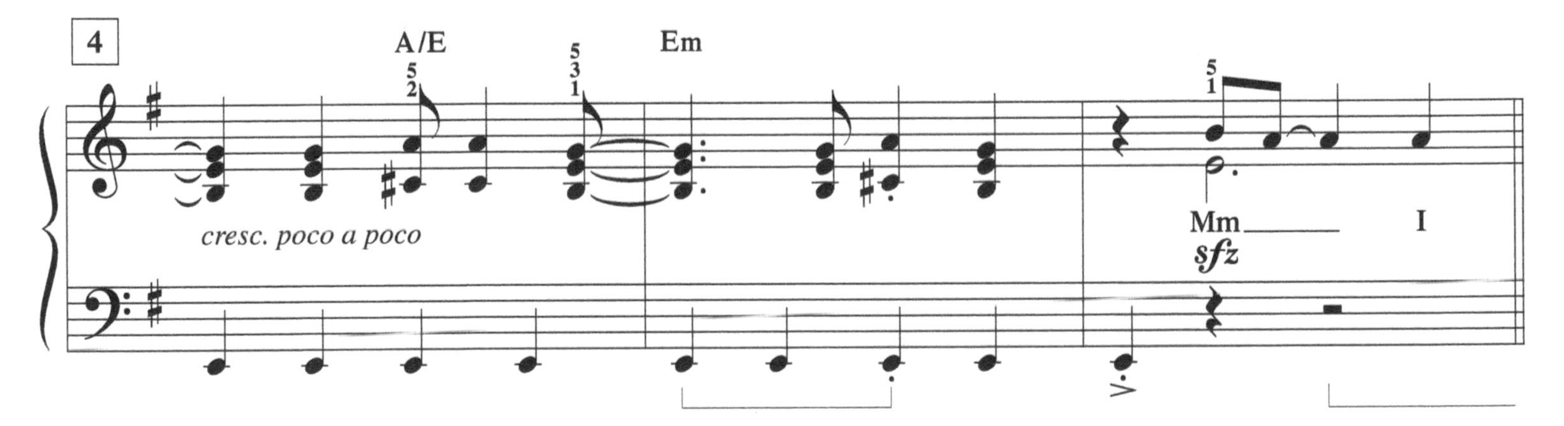

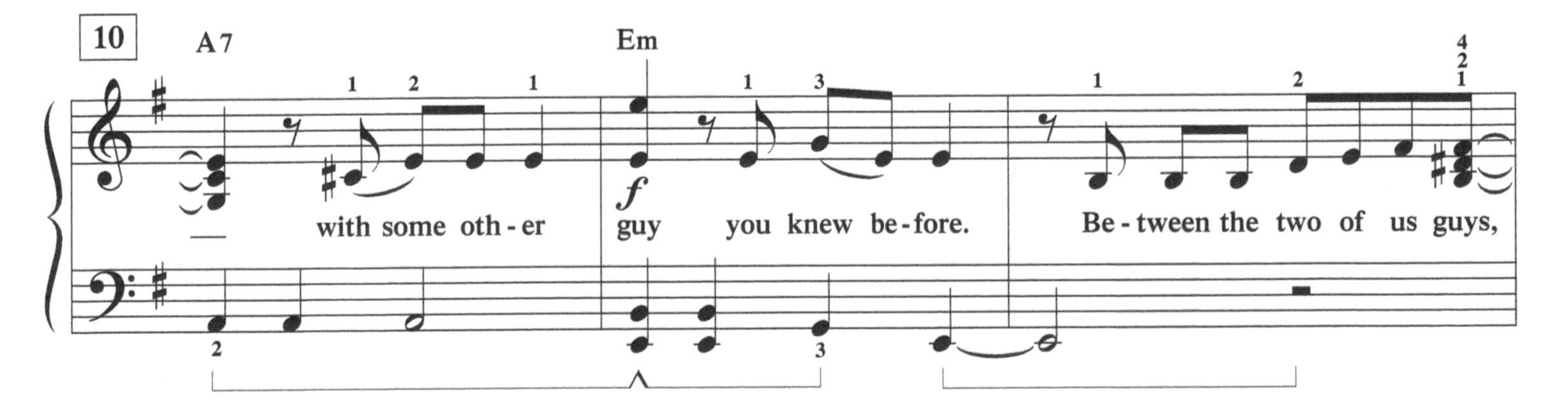

13
B
A7
C♯m
— you know I loved you more. — It took me by sur - prise, — I must
16
A7
Em7
A7
say, when I found out yes - ter-day. Don't you know that I heard
19
Em7
A7
it through the grape - vine, — not much — long - er would you be mine.
22
Em7
Oh, I heard — it through the grape - vine, — Oh, I'm
25
A7
just a - bout to lose — my mind. Hon - ey, hon - ey, I

27
Em
heard it through the grape - vine, not much long - er would you be mine, ba -
mp

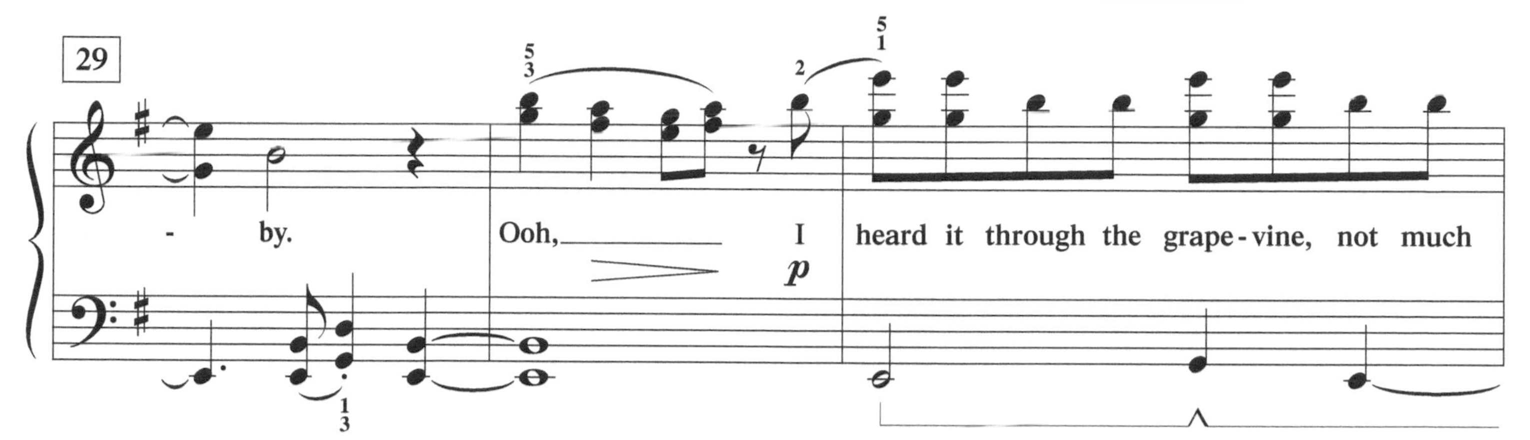
29
- by. Ooh, I heard it through the grape - vine, not much
p

32
long - er would you be mine, ba - by.

34
mp
cresc.

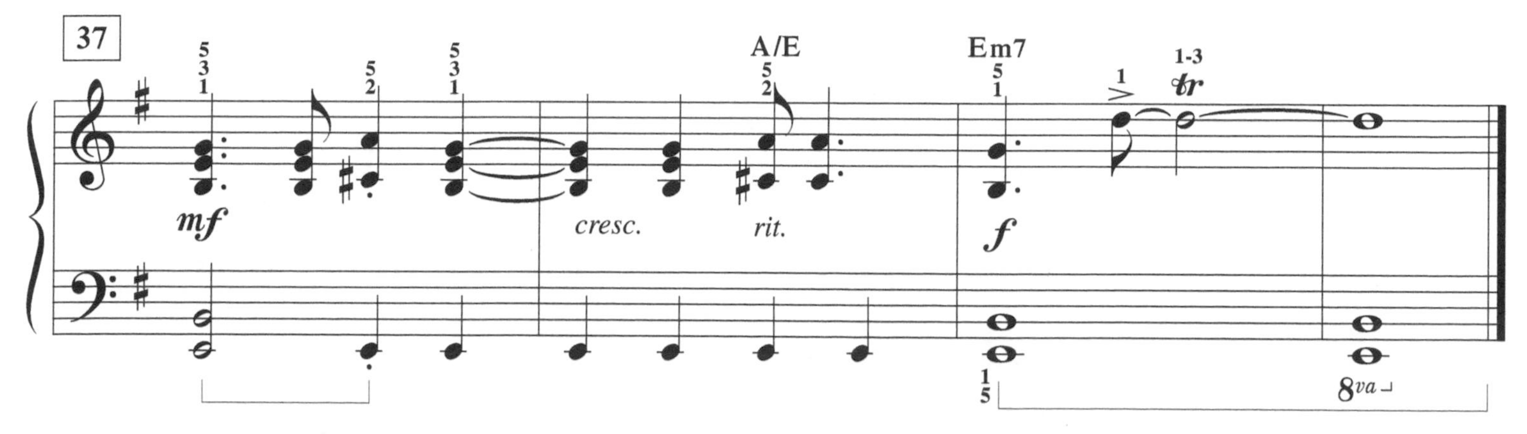
37
A/E
Em7
mf
cresc.
rit.
f
8va

Bad, Bad Leroy Brown

Words and Music by
JIM CROCE

Barrelhouse rock

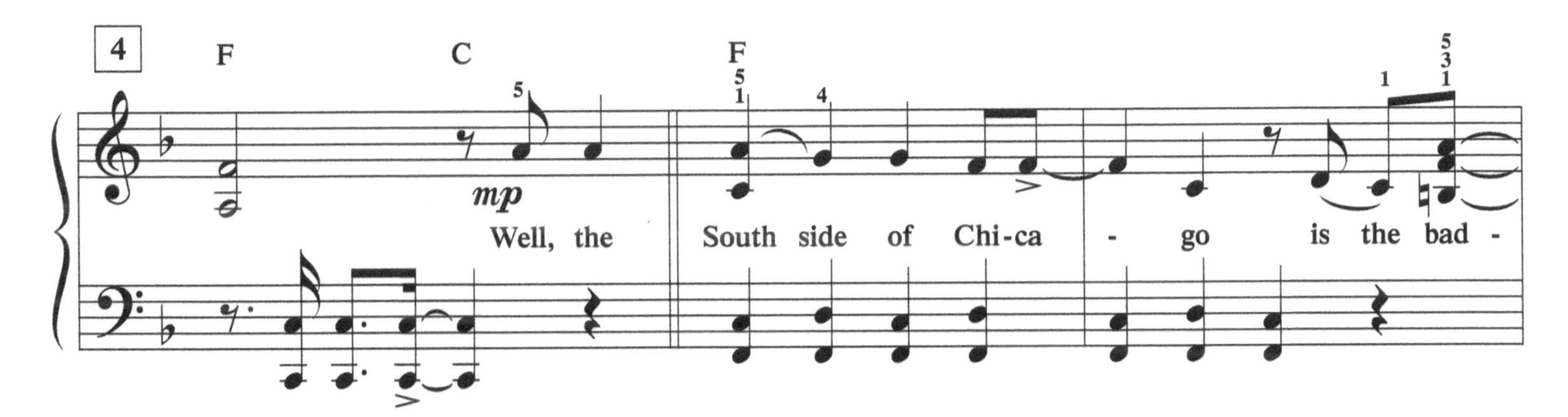

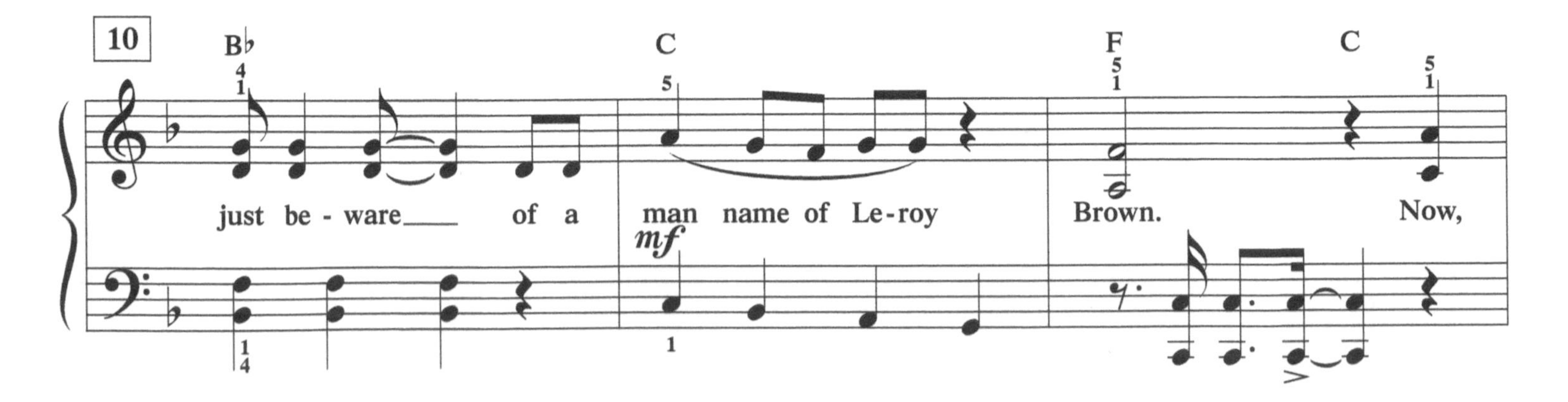

13
F
G7
Le - roy more than trou - ble. You see, he stand 'bout six foot four.
mp

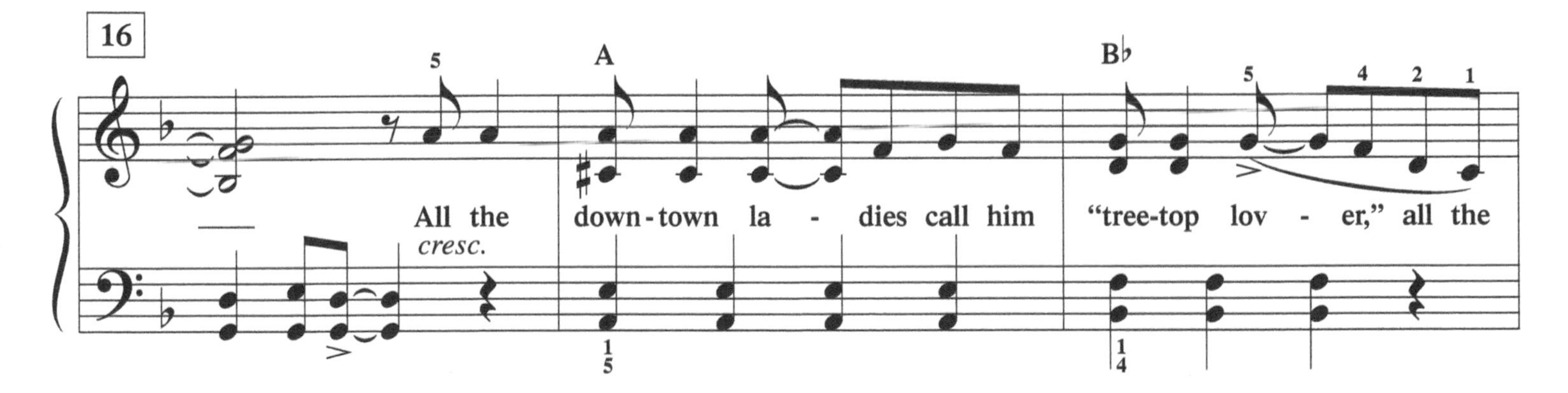
16
A
B♭
All the down - town la - dies call him "tree-top lov - er," all the
cresc.

19
C
F
C
F
mf
men just call him "sir." And he's bad, bad Le-roy Brown,
f

23
G7
A
bad - dest man in the whole damned town, bad-der than old King

26
B♭
C
1.
F
C
2.
F
Kong and mean-er than a junk-yard dog. And he's dog.
8va

I Feel the Earth Move

Words and Music by
CAROLE KING

Strong rock beat

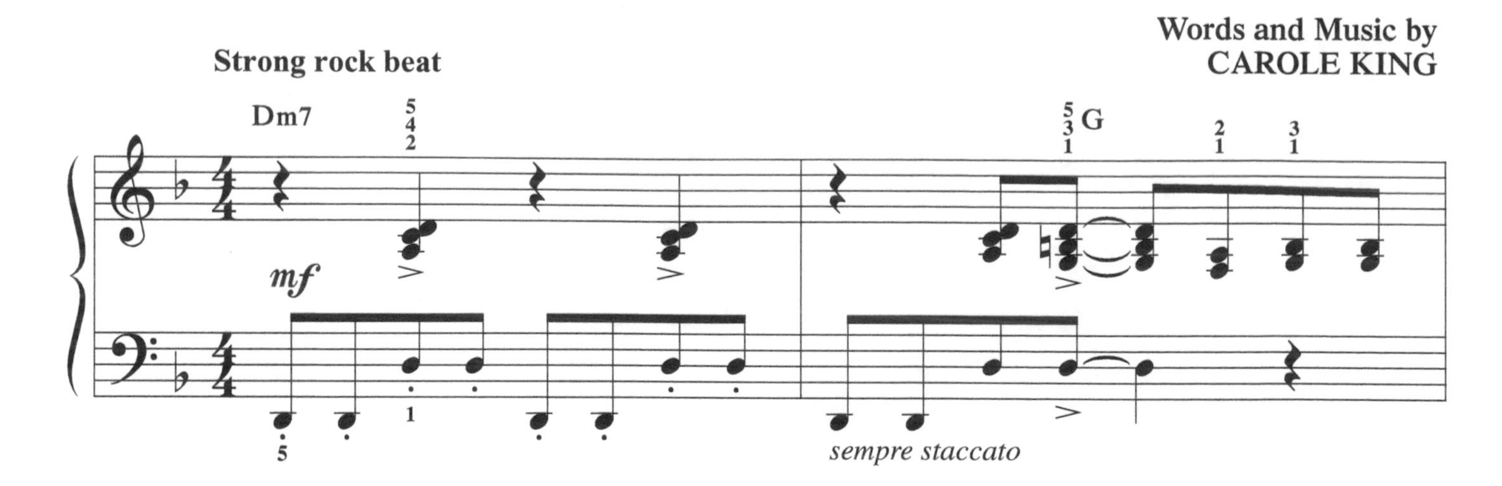

10
Dm7
when-ev - er you're a-round.
mf Ooh ba-

13
Fmaj7
B♭maj7
Gm9
- by, when I see your face
mel-low as the month of May,

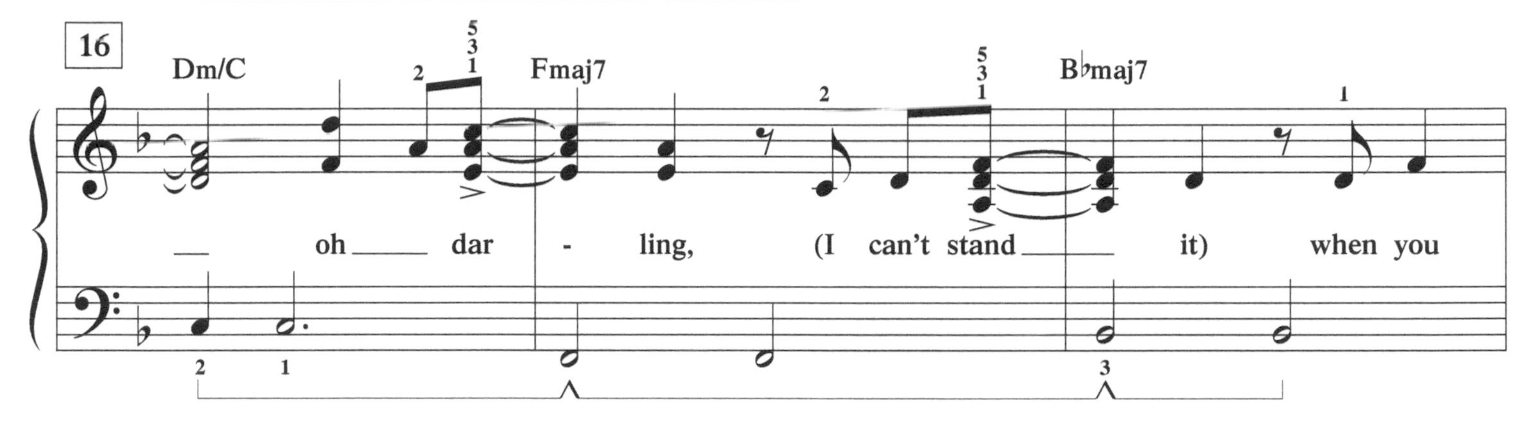

16
Dm/C
Fmaj7
B♭maj7
oh dar - ling, (I can't stand it) when you

19
Gm9
Dm/C
Dm7
look at me that a - way. Hey, I feel the
earth move

22
un - der my feet, I feel the
sky tum - bl' - ing down.

24
F/G
G7
I feel my heart start to trem-bl'-ing when-ev - er

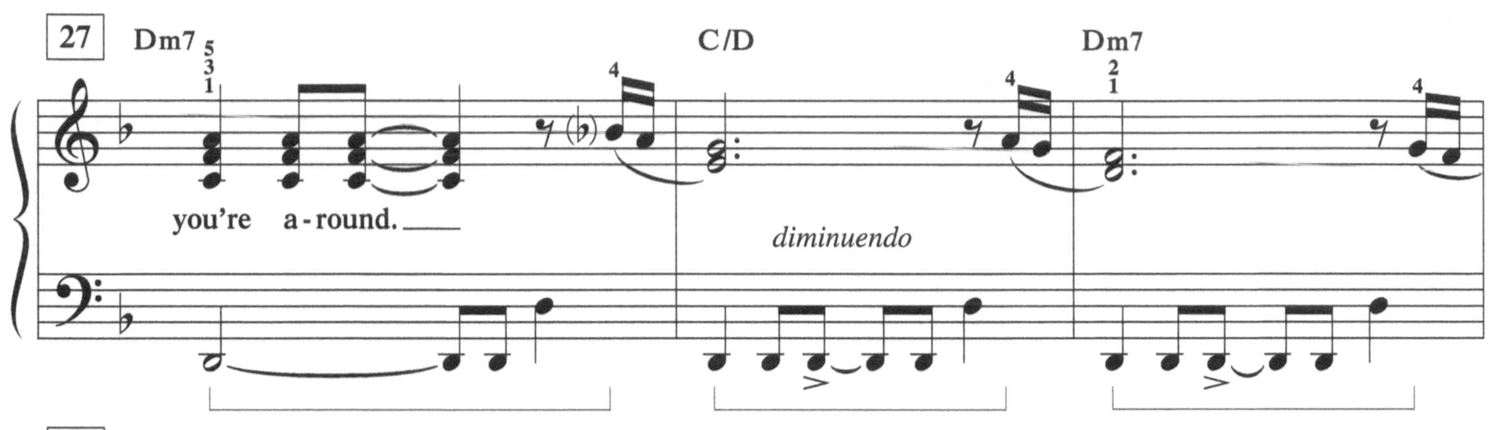
27
Dm7
C/D
Dm7
you're a-round.
diminuendo

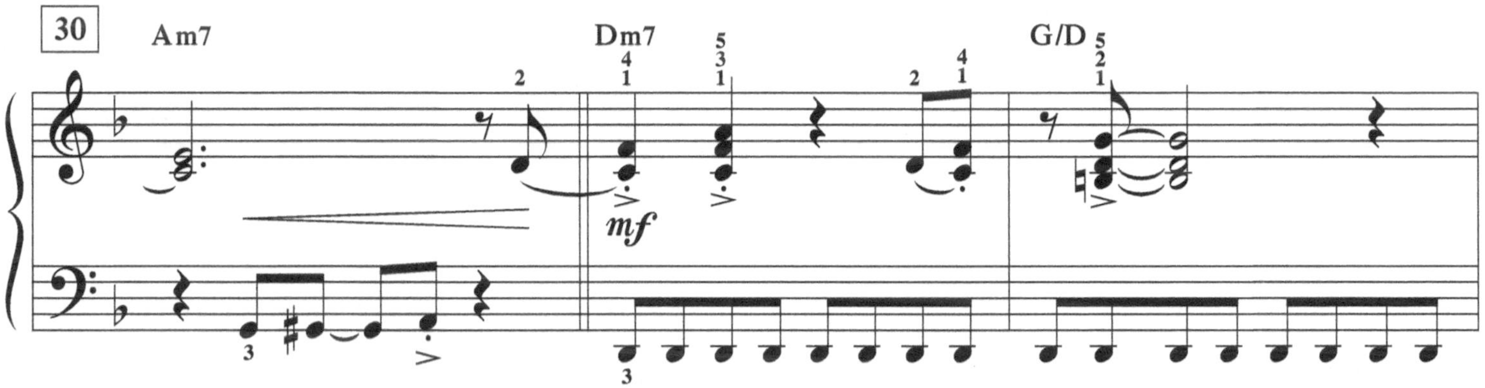
30
Am7
Dm7
G/D
mf

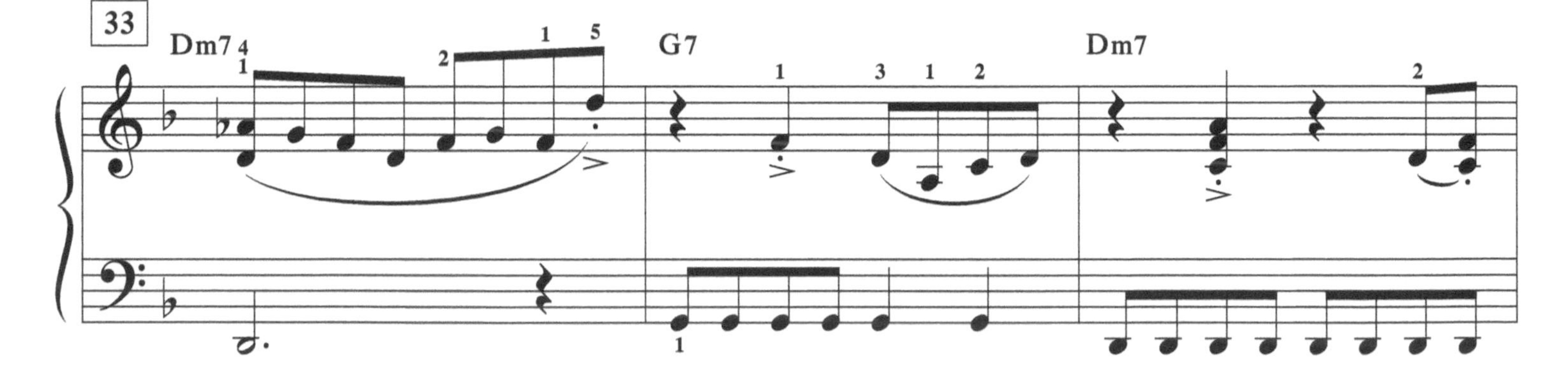
33
Dm7
G7
Dm7

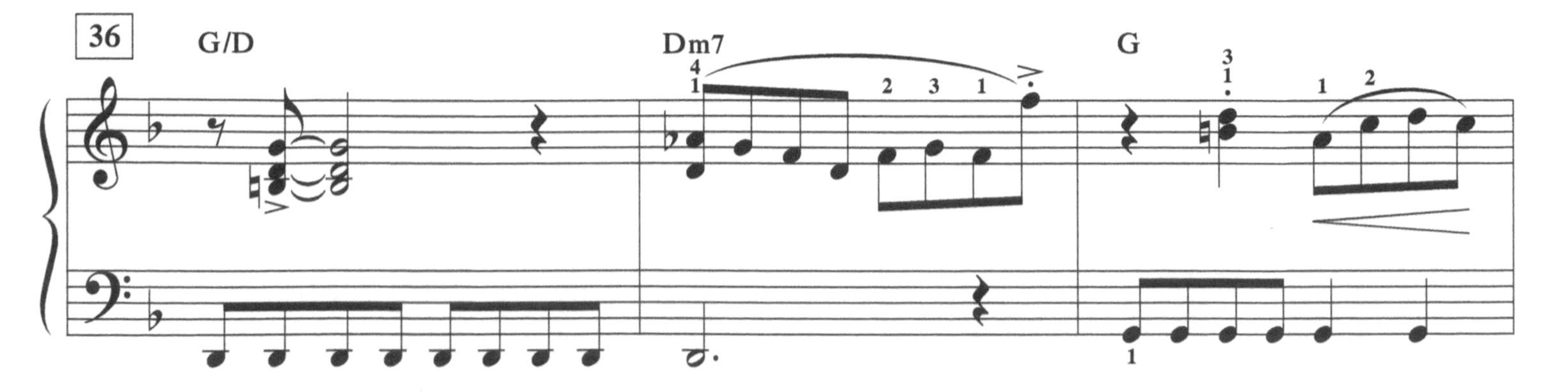
36
G/D
Dm7
G

39
Dm7
G7
Dm
f

42
G7
Dm7
Dm7/G

45
Dm7
G
Dm7
I feel the earth move
mf

48
un-der my feet, I feel the sky tum-bl'-ing down. tum-bl'-ing down, a-tum-bl'-
rit. poco a poco

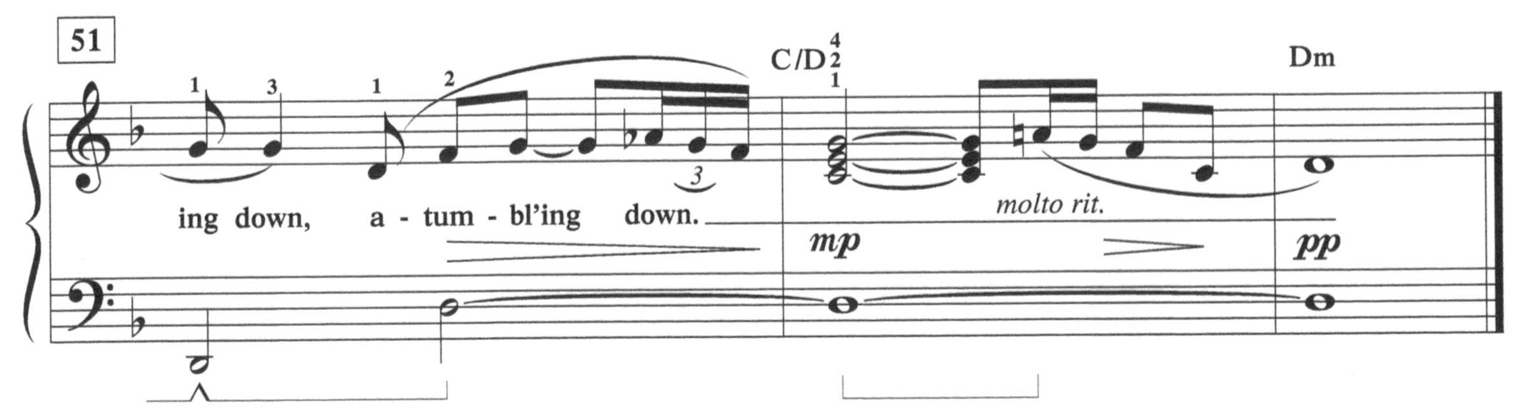
51
C/D
Dm
ing down, a-tum-bl'ing down.
mp
molto rit.
pp

Walk, Don't Run

Music by
JOHNNY SMITH

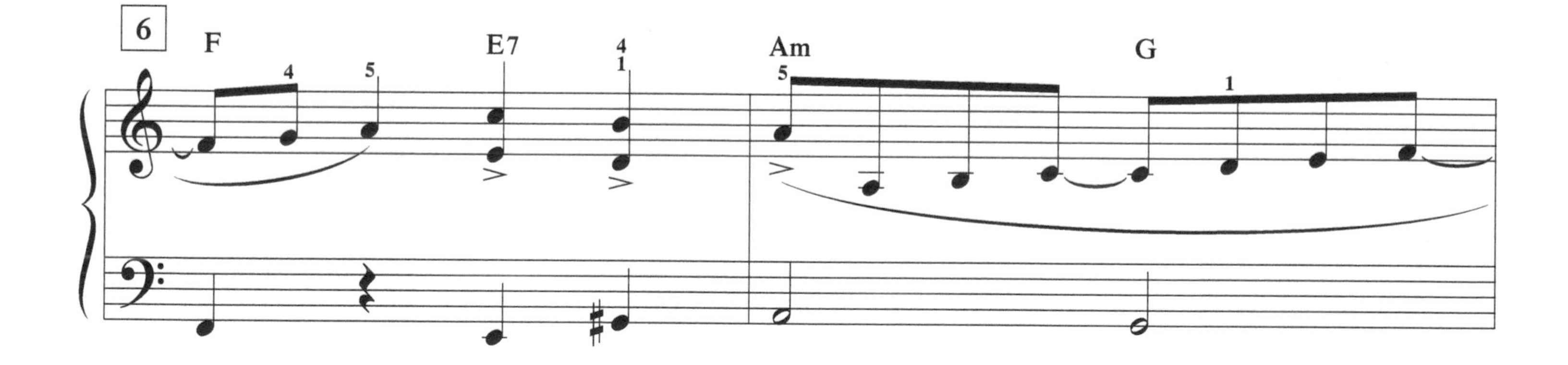

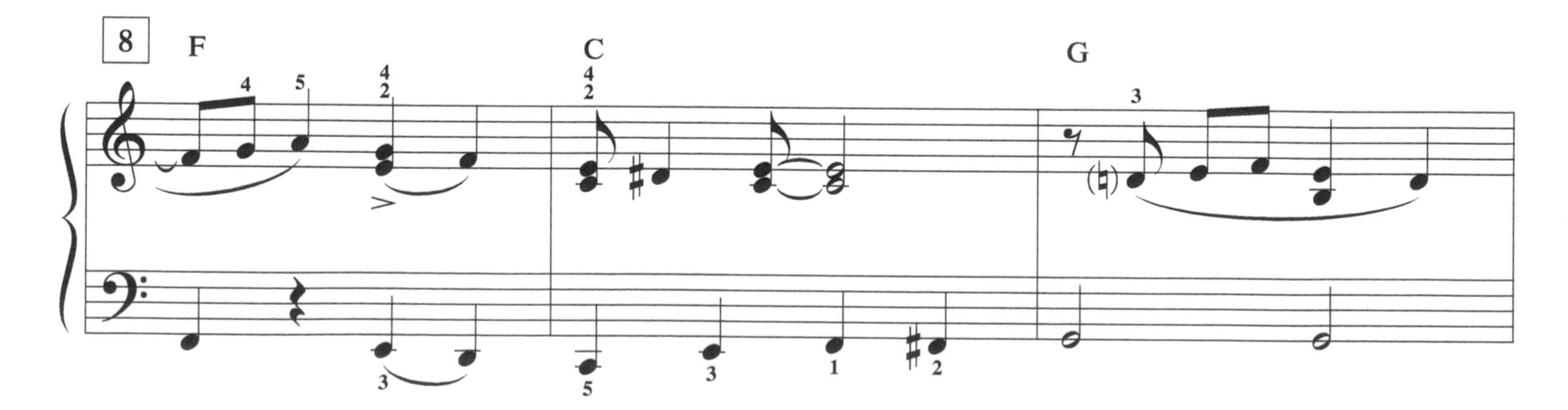

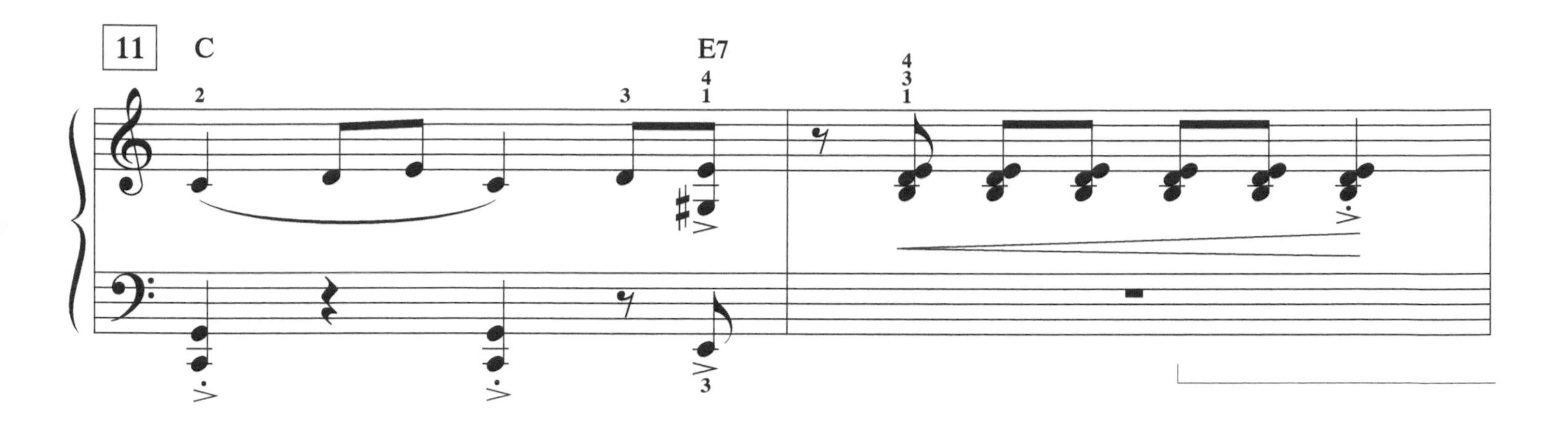
11
C
E7

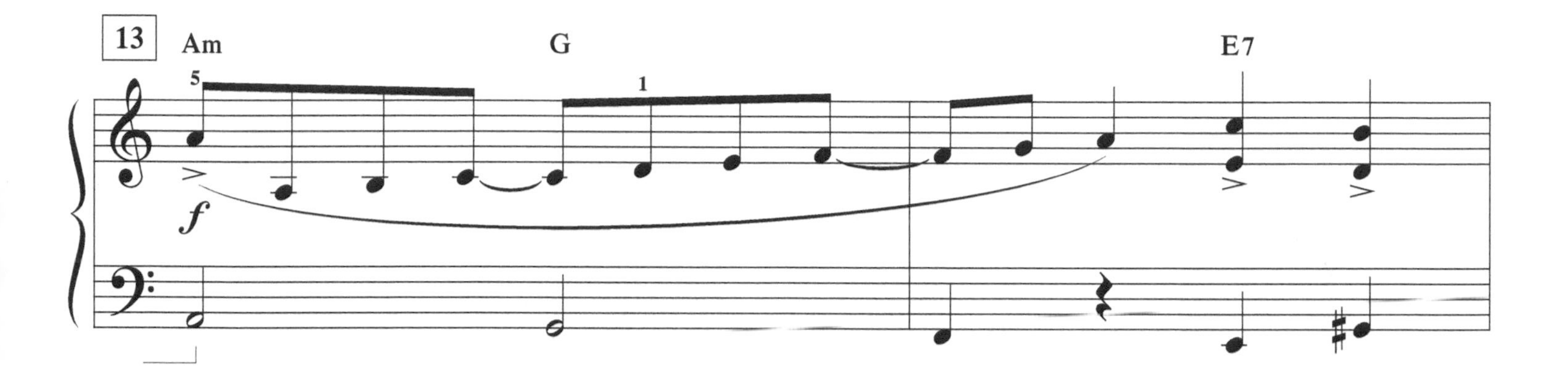
13
Am
G
E7
f

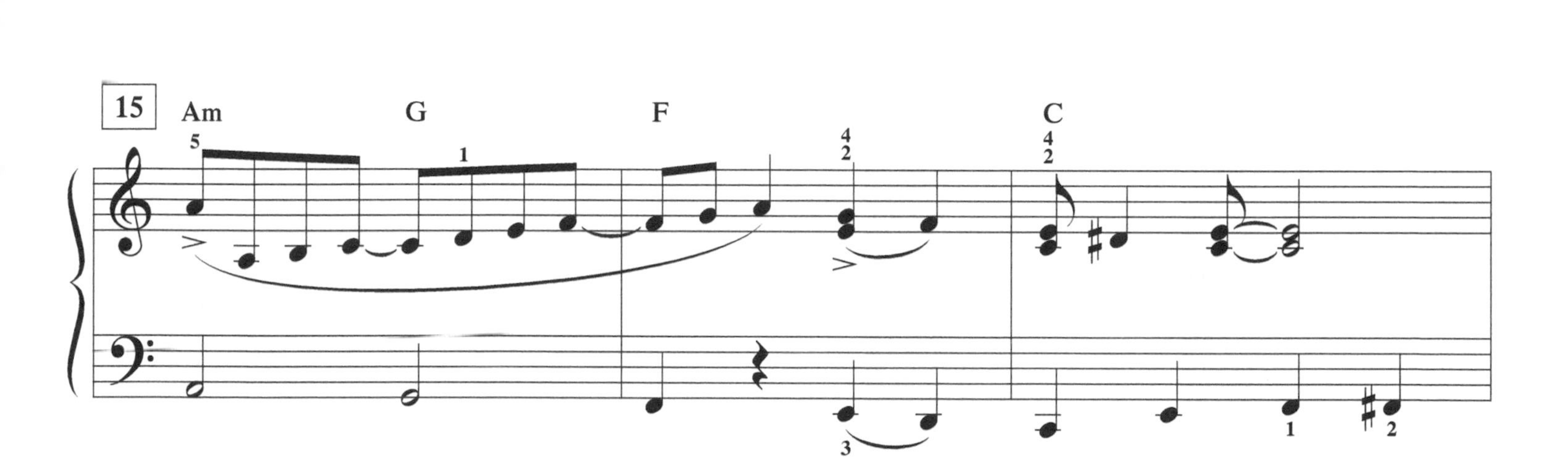
15
Am
G
F
C

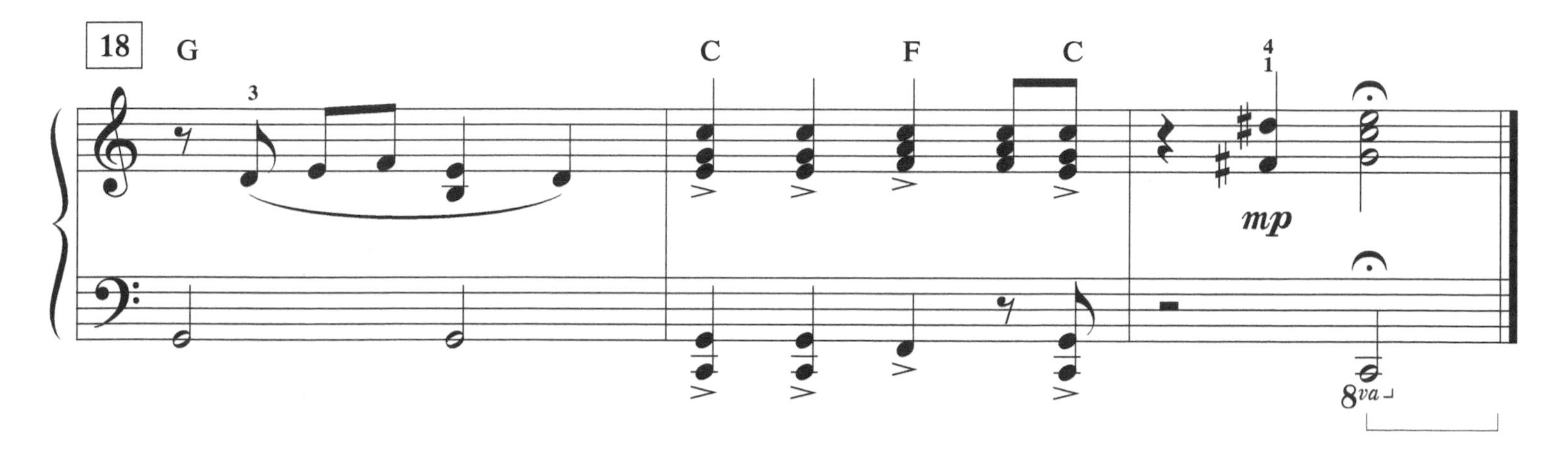
18
G
C
F
C
mp
8va

I May Have Lost My Girlfriend, But I've Still Got My Car

Lyrics by
JENNIFER MACLEAN

Music by
NANCY FABER and RANDALL FABER

11
B♭
A four - bar - rel car - bu - re - tor
But she was a lem - on and she

14
F
makes a bet - ter friend by far.
can't com - pare to what I've got.

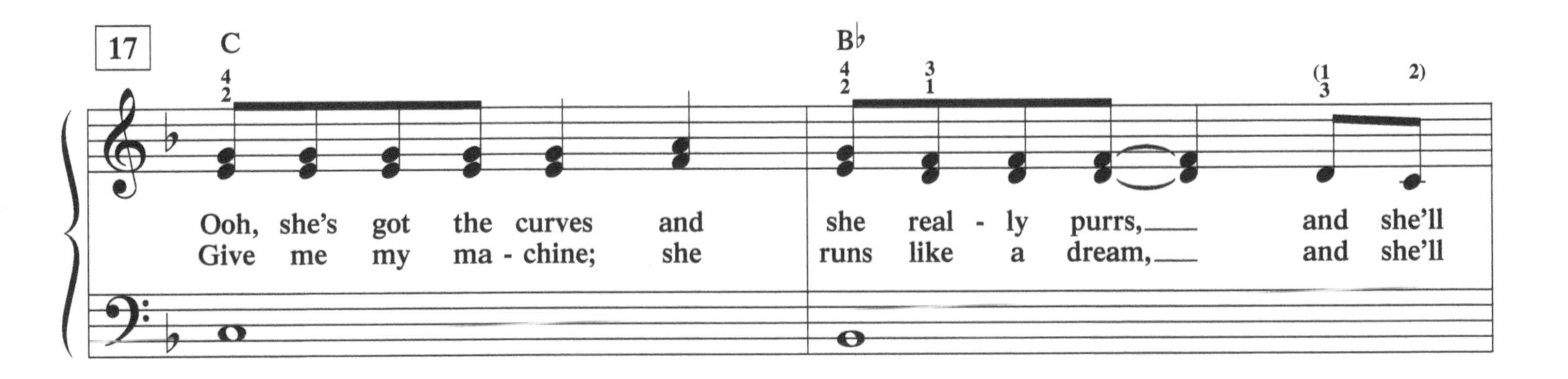
17
C
B♭
Ooh, she's got the curves and she real - ly purrs, and she'll
Give me my ma - chine; she runs like a dream, and she'll

19
F
E♭
E
F
1.
2.
nev - er break up with me!

22
F6
f

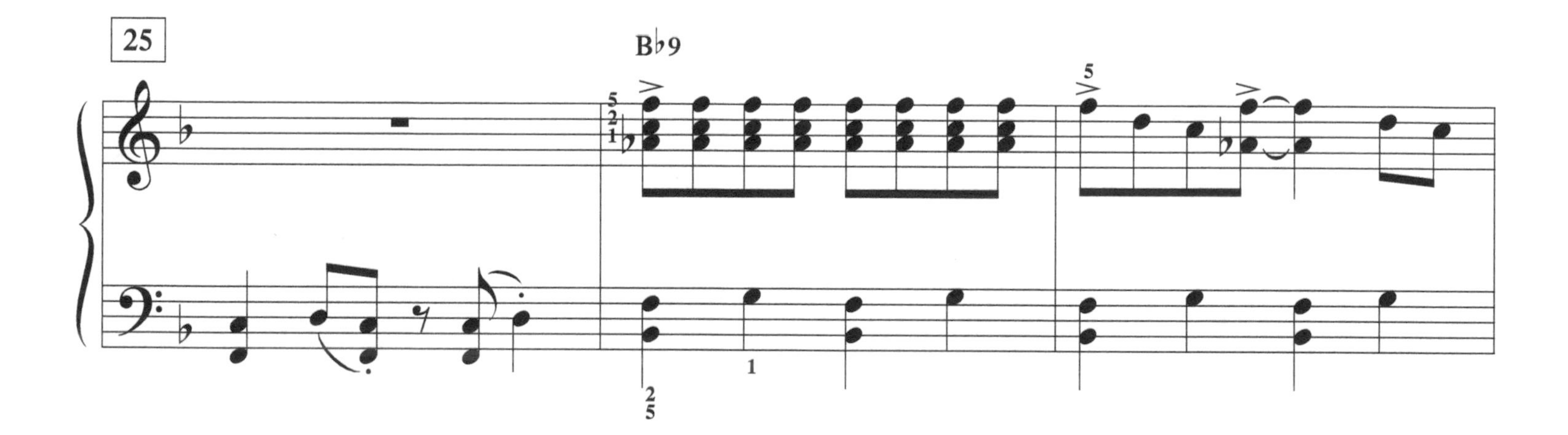
25
B♭9

28
F
Cm7

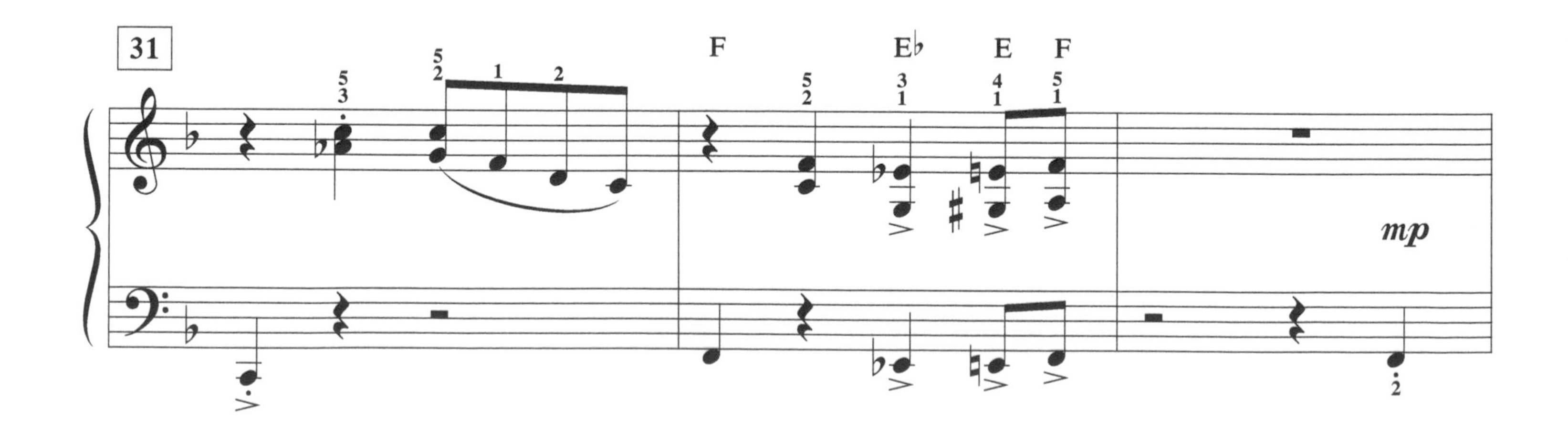
31
F
E♭
E
F
mp

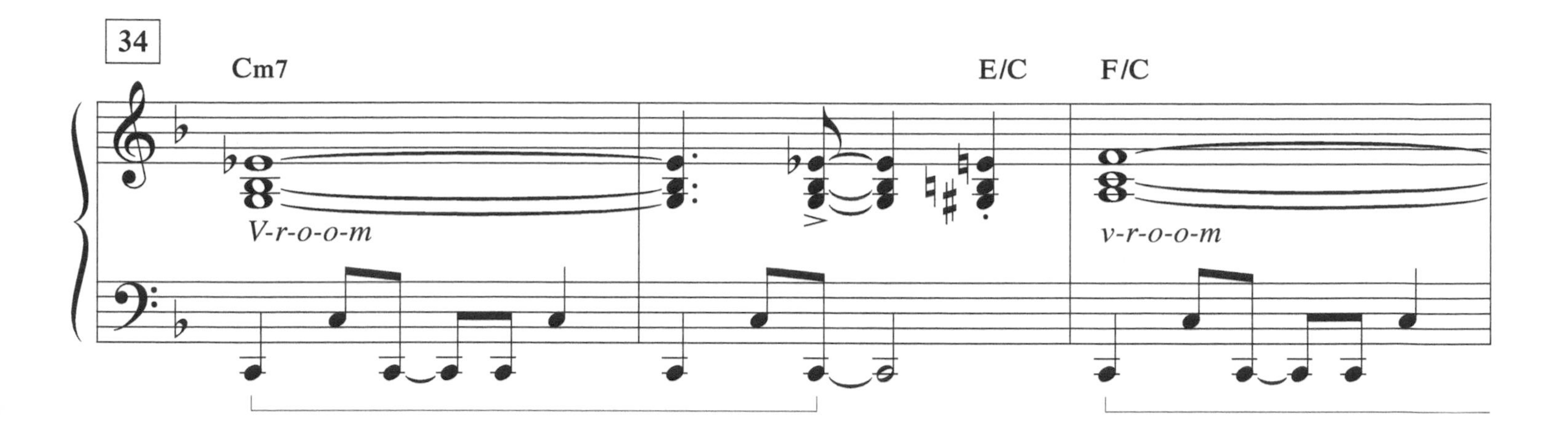
34
Cm7
E/C
F/C
V-r-o-o-m
v-r-o-o-m

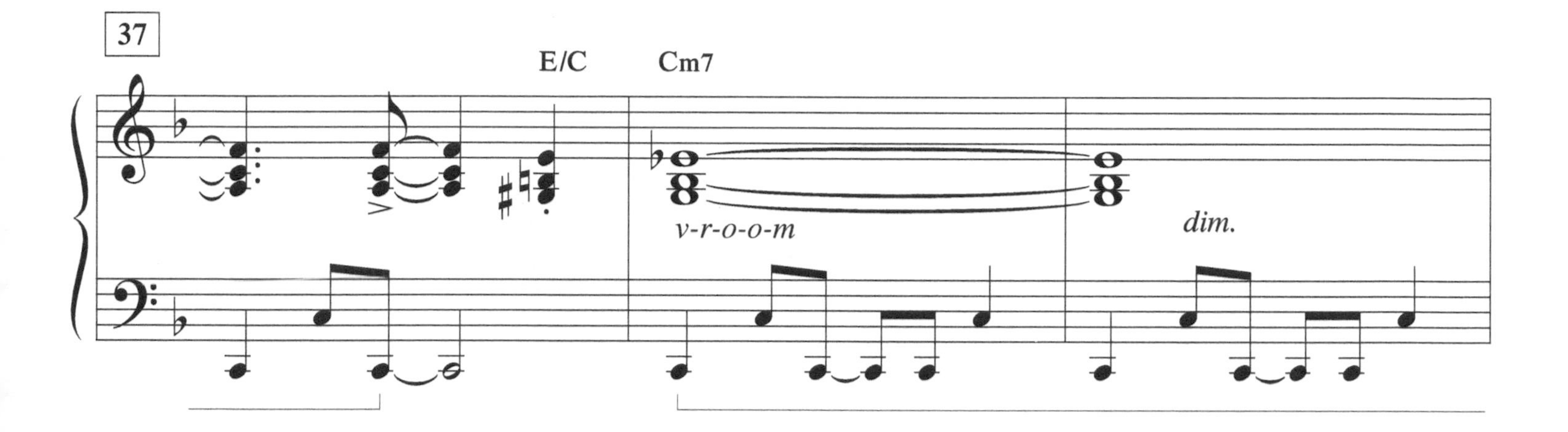
37
E/C
Cm7
v-r-o-o-m
dim.

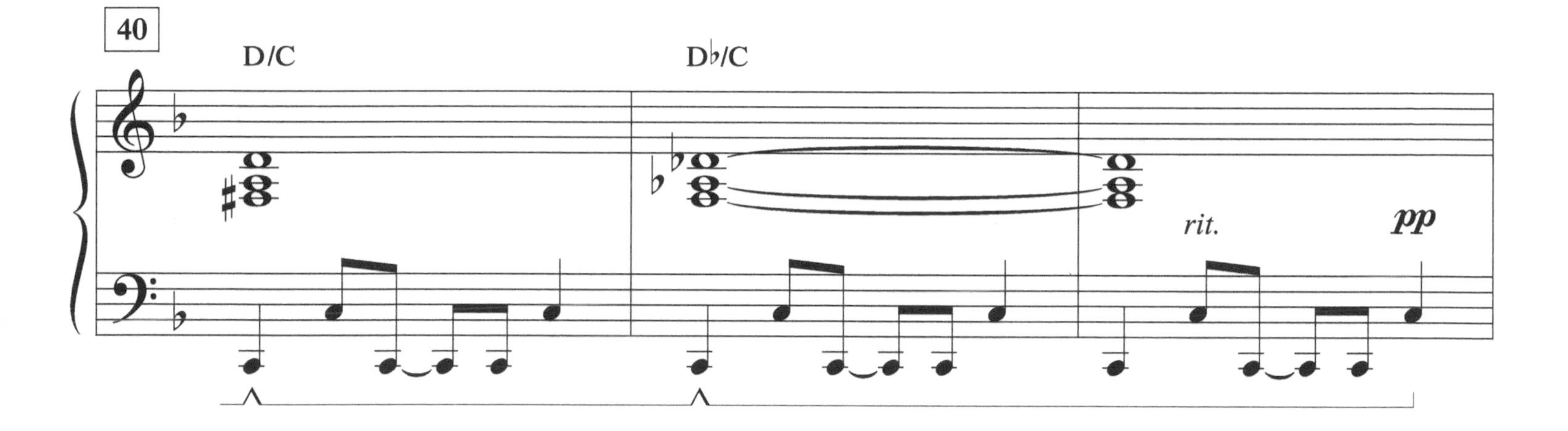
40
D/C
D♭/C
rit.
pp

43
F7
ff
a tempo
rit.
sfz

The Game of Love

CLINT BALLARD Jr.

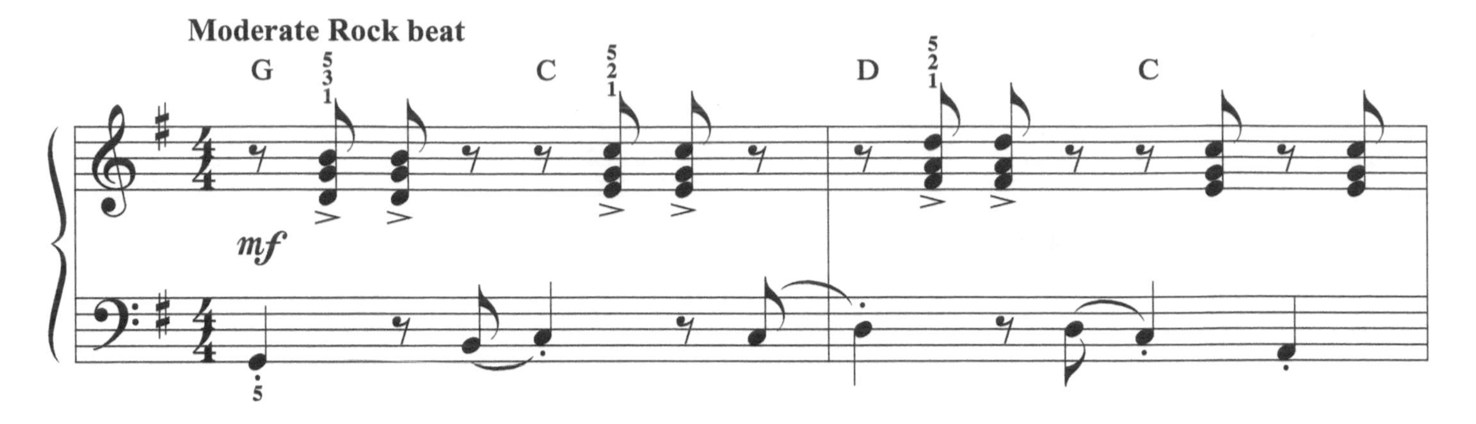

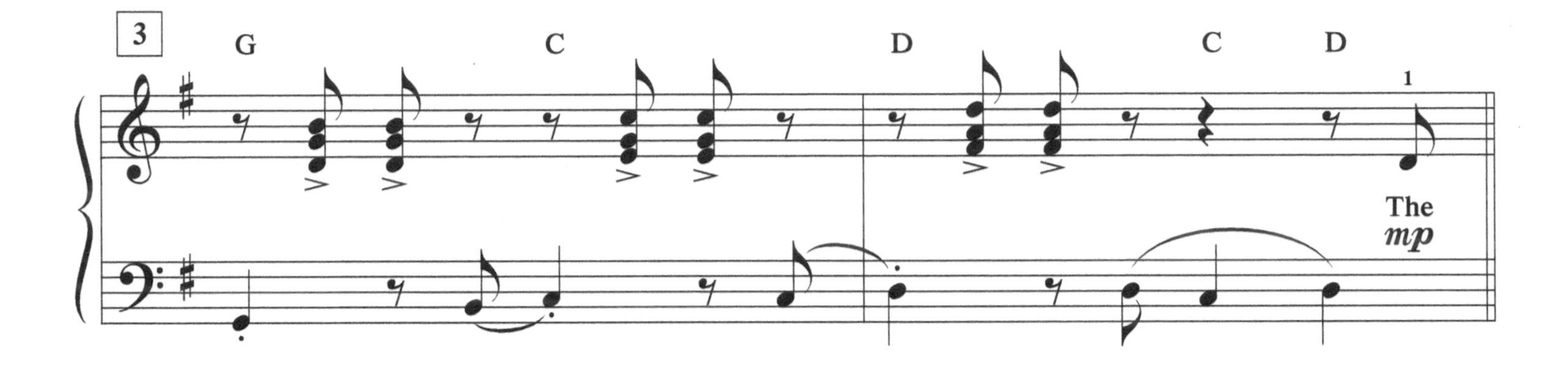

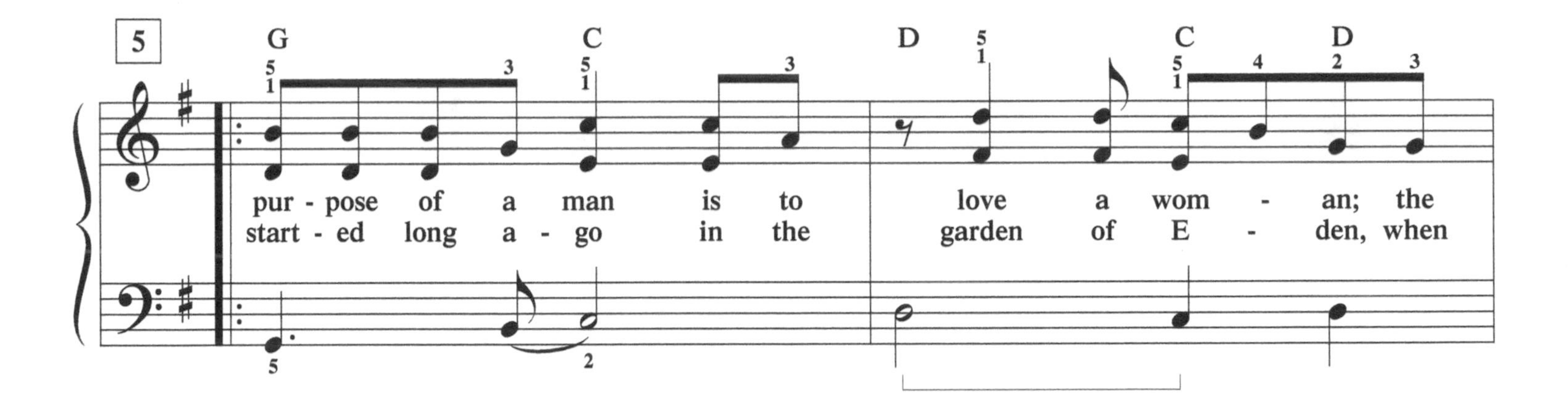

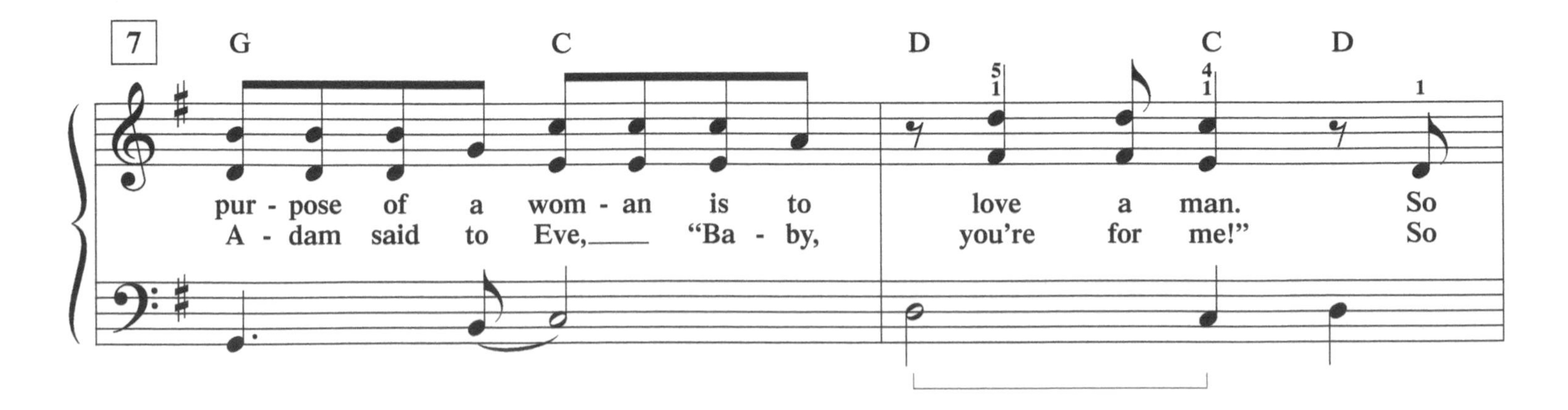

9
G C A7 D
come on, ba - by, it's here to stay, come on, ba - by, let's play the game of
come on, ba - by, it's still the same, come on, ba - by, let's play the game of
cresc.
mf

11
1.
G C A7 D
love, love, love, love, la la la la la love! It
mp

13
2.
G C A7 D
love, love, love, love, la la la la la love! Hey,
f

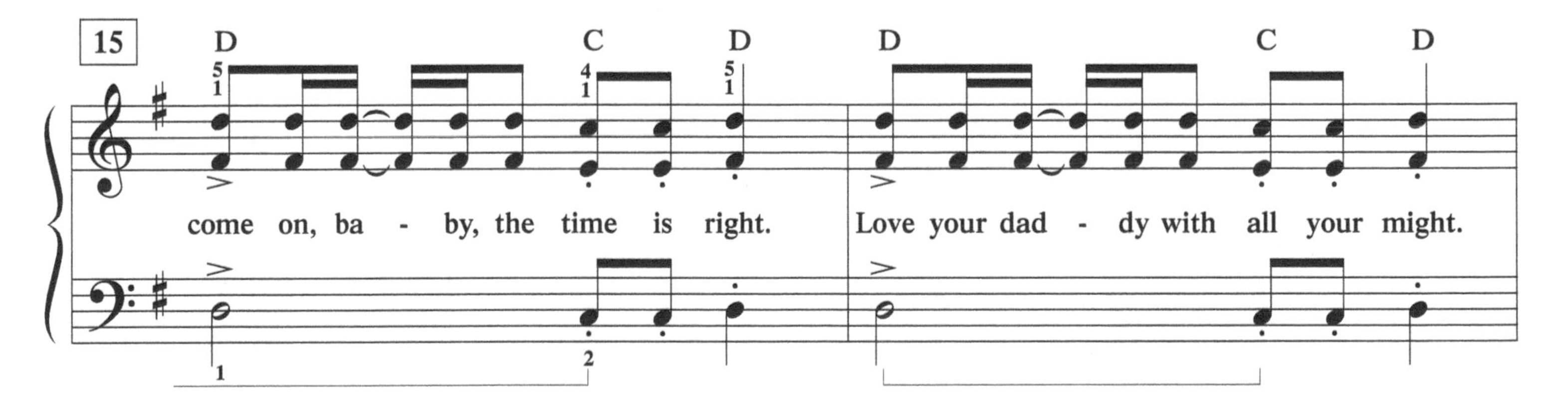
15
D C D D C D
come on, ba - by, the time is right. Love your dad - dy with all your might.

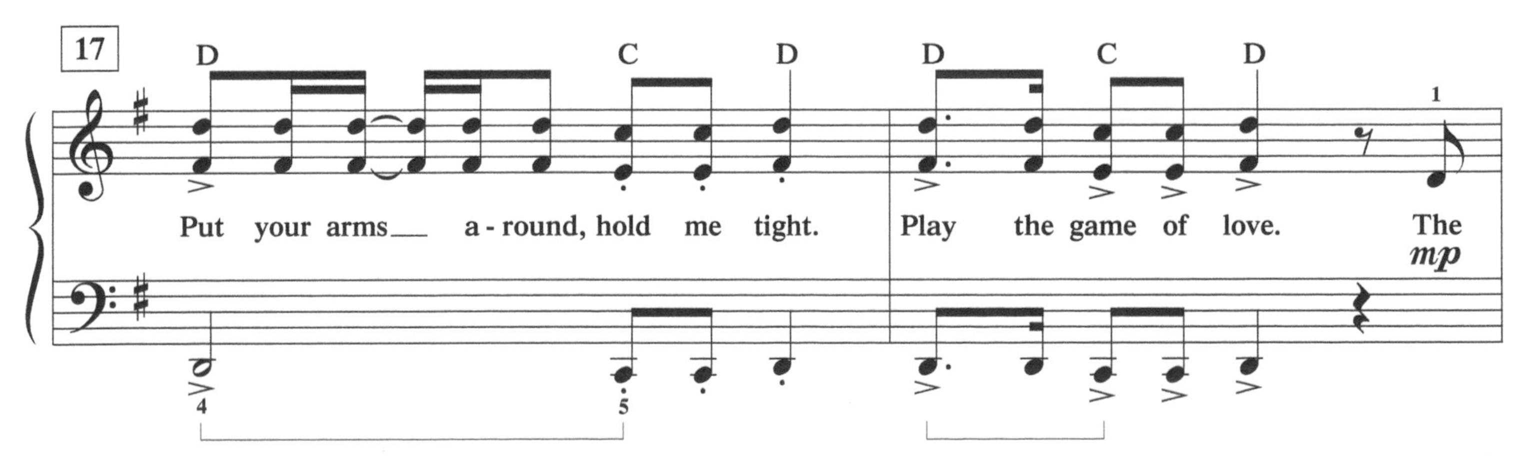
17
D C D D C D
Put your arms a - round, hold me tight. Play the game of love. The
mp

19
G C D C D
pur - pose of a man is to love a wom - an; the
L.H.
8va
21
G C D C D
pur - pose of a wom - an is to love a man. So
(8va)
23
G C A7 D
come on, ba - by, it's here to stay, come on, ba - by, let's play the game of
cresc.
mf
(8va)

25
G C A7 D G C
love, love, love, love, la la la la la love! The game of love, love, love, love,
f
(8va)

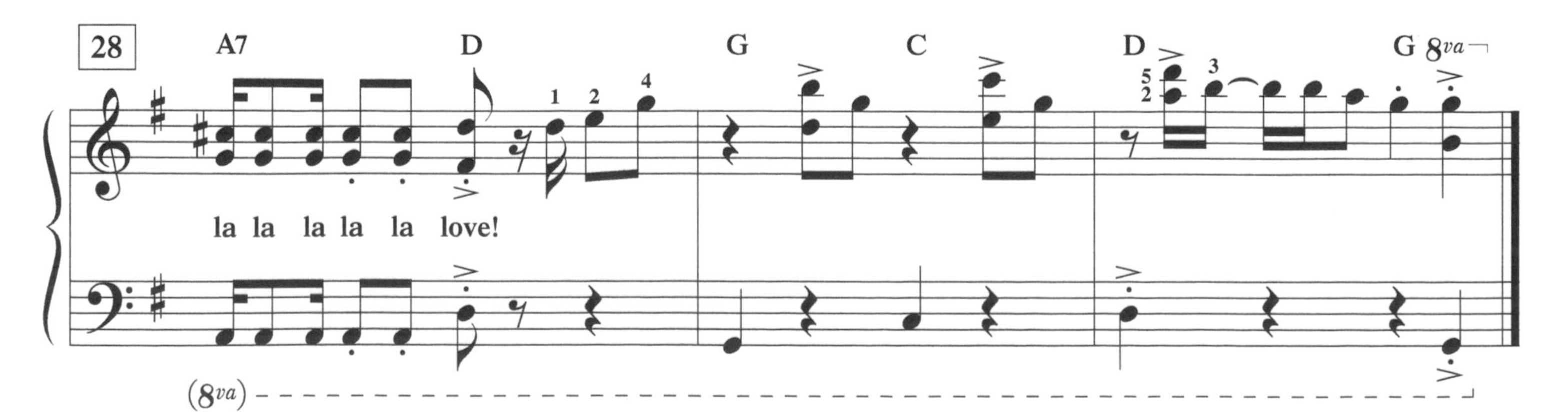
28
A7 D G C D G
8va
la la la la la love!
(8va)